Making a Welcome

MAKING A WELCOME

Christian Life and the Practice of Hospitality

Maria Poggi Johnson

CASCADE *Books* · Eugene, Oregon

MAKING A WELCOME
Christian Life and the Practice of Hospitality

Cascade Books
An Imprint of Wipf and Stock Publishers
199 W. 8th Ave., Suite 3
Eugene, OR 97401

www.wipfandstock.com

ISBN 13: 978-1-61097-471-4

Cataloging-in-Publication data:

Johnson, Maria Poggi.

    Making a welcome : Christian life and the practice of hospitality
/ Maria Poggi Johnson.

    x + 114 p. ; 23 cm. —Includes bibliographical references.

    ISBN 13: 978-1-61097-471-4

    1. Hospitality — Religious aspects — Christianity. I. Title.

BV4647.H67 J62 2011

Manufactured in the U.S.A.

*To my children, Catherine, Elisabeth, Adam and Laura
with love and thanks for their extraordinary tolerance and
humor about living in Grand Central Station.*

As a house at all times freely open, much frequented, of great haunt, and officious in entertaining all sorts of people (for I could never bee induced to make an implement of warre thereof; which I perceive much more willingly to bee sought out and flocked unto where it is furthest from my neighbours) my house hath merited much popular affection.

—Michel de Montaigne, *Of Vanitie*

Contents

Acknowledgments

This book was written during a sabbatical, funded in part by a Christian Faith and Life Grant from the Louisville Institute: my thanks go to Jim Lewis and the Institute, and to Dean Paul Fahey, who allowed me the year I needed for the work. I am very grateful to my department, for being a wonderful place to work, and in particular to Charlie Pinches for guidance both honest and encouraging, and for steering me to Cascade, where I am delighted to have found a home for this book and the help and support of Charlie Collier. Special thanks to Beth McManus for synthesizing a couple decades of philosophical study into a couple of evenings. Thanks to Michael Atlin for technical help.

My deepest debt is to those people from and with whom I have learned about welcome over many years. There are far more of them than I can hope to mention here; hardly anybody with whom I have ever shared an evening or a meal from whom I have not learned something. But of course some stand out: my father Gian Poggi and his wife, Marcella; Gabriella Poggi; Marzio and Donatella Barbagli; Sarah Farrimond and her family; the Johnson family; Dan and Amy Lloyd; Stephen and Jenny Whittaker; the Strange Boys; the Damn Alcoholics; the Gay Archers; Hipsters for Jesus; and everybody who knows not to bother knocking.

My husband Glen has been a constant presence, a fellow adventurer in the noisy business of keeping an open house, and a staunch support through the essentially solitary travails of book-writing. I couldn't have done—and can't do—much of any-thing without him.

Introduction

Cheap Chocolate for the Guests

Leaving an event at the university the other night, my husband and I stopped to talk to Robby, whom we had met when he was a freshman in my intro class. He told us that he was on his way to a hot tub party with some girls from his old high school. An hour later he materialized in the living room (people rarely knock) with his guitar and a slightly dazed expression.

"Hey you, what brings you here? Weren't you going to a party?"

"Well I knew it would be a really bad idea, so here I am, and I think I must be out of my mind." He stumped into the kitchen, banged around a bit, returned with a couple of fried-egg sandwiches and a cup of tea, flopped onto the sofa and stayed there until the small hours playing us Neil Young and Tom Waits and shaking his head in bewilderment at his own folly.

This story really starts twenty years ago. I was in my last year at Oxford; possibly the happiest of three extraordinarily happy years. Of course nostalgia has a tendency to drench things in syrupy golden light, but I was acutely aware at the time that I was wildly, giddily happy. Oxford itself doesn't need nostalgia to make it glow. It is ancient and lovely and steeped in wisdom and we were young and clever and fizzing with delight, at large among cloisters and libraries and gardens that, for the space of a deep and glorious breath, belonged only to us. It was glorious, but it was a lot of work, leading up to a week of six-hour exams on which our degrees (and our lives, it seemed at the time) hung. Sarah and Phil and I, feeling frazzled, had invited ourselves to Joe and Linette's for the weekend. Being well-brought-up young things we had stopped at the posh chocolate shop on our way to catch the bus, and when we got to the house, we presented them with one of those elegant little boxes you get in posh chocolate shops with about six very high-end truffles.

"Ooh, super!" said Linette. "We *love* these." Then she rifled through a pile of books and papers, pulled open a couple of drawers and poked around inside them, looked under some cushions, and eventually produced a rather battered, dusty box of cheap supermarket chocolates which she handed to us, saying, "Here, look, you have these ones." Then we all sat down and ate our respective chocolates, and I was as happy as I have ever been.

We had met Joe and Linette earlier in the year when our college Christian Union went to their house for a study weekend. Joe led Bible study sessions, Linette fed us. Then I went back with other friends and with just Sarah. I don't think I went above three or four times—I can't have spent more than ten days there at the most—but it changed my life. It was like falling in love, but not the way I was in love with Oxford: a heady romantic rapture that I knew, even when I was dizzy with bliss, was bound to burn itself out sooner or later. This was like meeting someone and realizing that they undoubtedly stack dishes all wrong and have hideous taste in films, and that you want to spend the rest of your life with them and have their babies and that's that.

They lived in an old farmhouse with a number of add-ons, in the countryside near Oxford. The place was a mess. Not like the houses of those dreadful people who simper "oh please ignore the mess" when the mess you are supposed to ignore consists of a couple of toddlers' books, a teddy bear and a stray plate with a few crumbs on it. Joe and Linette's mess was deep, heartfelt, and enduring. Every inch of the downstairs was a morass of gardening shoes and tools and cats and lumpy plastic bags full of heaven knows what and papers and books and books and books in no sort of order, in piles and stacks and puddles. Upstairs there was a bare, chilly corridor lined with bare, chilly, slightly clammy rooms each with as many battered bunk beds as could be made to fit.

It was a long way from the glamor of Oxford, but it was a perfect house, because of Joe and Linette's extraordinary hospitality. It seemed as if they had undertaken a rigorous Cartesian program of jettisoning and rethinking every cliché, convention, or assumption about what really makes people enjoy themselves when they come to stay. What makes a visit fun? Well, of course you'd like really good food. There it was: plentiful, unfussy, and delicious. I had my first tabouli there, tingling with parsley from the garden that Linette was building, one muddy plot at a time, from pictures in medieval manuscripts.

Everybody wants to eat well, but nobody really wants to chop carrots or wash dishes. The kitchen was strictly out of bounds; Linette became quite ferocious if you so much as tried to carry your own plate to the kitchen. In fact there were no chores at all, certainly none of those soul-chilling lists of tasks that are the first thing you encounter in many British retreat centers: "Notice to our guests; before you leave please put all your linen into the pillow case and put it in the yellow basket outside the bathroom. Turn the radiator knob 170 degrees counterclockwise. Take the contents of your wastebasket to the green trash bin behind the kitchen door, etc. etc. etc."

In particular you want to be able to relax, without having to worry about whether you are supposed to entertain your host or to allow yourself to be entertained, or about whether you are talking too much or too little according to some standard that is never quite made clear. Around Joe and Linette one never worried, because they clearly didn't. Sometimes they'd interrupt conversations and tell stories and ask nosey questions; sometimes they'd go about their business and let us fend for ourselves until we were called to table. Linette didn't much care for the ritual of "goodbye, thanks ever so much, we had a lovely time," "oh it was pleasure to have you, please come back any time" and was generally nowhere to be found when we left.

And when we brought fancy chocolates they guzzled them down with obvious relish and gave us the cheap ones and nothing they could possibly have done would have made us feel more welcome. The stuff we brought was really good and we all knew it. They wanted it all for themselves, and they wanted it right then, and we knew that too. Who wouldn't? Had they put it aside murmuring that they would "enjoy it later" or, worse, shared it with us, we all would have been aware that the ethos of the house required that one make oneself uncomfortable for the sake of manners, and that we were supposed to do the same.

But because Joe and Linette always appeared to do exactly what they wanted to do, we felt we could too: put our feet on the furniture, root through their bookcases, keep them up talking till indecent hours, ignore them and do our own thing, eat a huge meal then stroll away from the devastation of the table and go for a walk by moonlight. We were being pampered as assiduously by the scruffy couple in the muddy shoes as we would have been by the white-jacketed staff of some preposterous luxury resort, but it never occurred to us that we were putting them to any trouble. This was nonsense, of course. Having a pack of students descending on your house for the weekend and not asking them to help with the chores creates a simply huge amount of work. I know, with adult hindsight, that Joe and Linette must have collapsed on many a Sunday night groaning, "Oh I've *had* it. Please tell me we haven't got another lot for a few weeks?" But we, inexperienced and innocently selfish, had no notion.

Part of why I was so deeply enamored of Joe and Linette's house was that it was altogether different from the one I grew up in. My mother—who was generous and adventurous and creative and warm and great fun in all sorts of other ways—was terribly stuffy and overanxious when it came to entertaining. She had acquired from somewhere or other a notion of how things had to be done if anybody but immediate family was in the house, and a near-apocalyptic sense of what would happen if they weren't done just that way. If there were people coming for dinner she fretted and fussed for days ahead of time and was exhausted afterwards, and we didn't do it very much at all. The idea that you could have people over when the plates didn't match and there were three-month-old newspapers under the dining room table and that not only would you not be struck by lightning, but everybody would have a great time came as a revelation to me, and opened up possibilities that have hugely shaped my adult life.

When my husband and I were "courting" I told him about Joe and Linette and how much I wanted to be like them. He was immediately on board, and we promised ourselves eagerly that as soon as we got out of grad school and one of us got a job we'd buy a cabin in Glen's beloved northern Minnesota woods and fill it with bunk beds and beanbags and tin plates. Then for a couple of months every summer we would take our favorite students there. Glen would take them hiking and canoeing, I would putter around (I don't really do outdoors) and have mounds of hot food ready for them when they came back and then we'd read and talk and sing and play Monopoly into the night.

The details of this plan, it turned out, were dependent on a hilariously unrealistic view of adult economics. Subsisting as graduate students on not very much at all, we thought of the salary of an assistant professor as untold riches and assumed that we'd easily be able to save enough in a couple of years to buy the cabin and the bean bags and the plates and get started. Suffice it to say that we were wrong, and the details had to go by the wayside. The spirit of the plan pretty much endures, however, translated into an idiom that has developed with us and our marriage. We have a big, old, shabby house (I can't claim quite the same standards of mess as Joe and Linette, but it's pretty close) four blocks from campus and there's a lot of people here, a lot of the time.

So we didn't think it the least bit odd when Robby showed up on the doorstep. He's always around: actually as I write this—at 2 a.m.—he's sitting on the other sofa, humming along to Pete Seeger on YouTube and just getting started on a paper that's due in seven hours. His sidekick, the taciturn banjo-playing math whiz Paul, the anarchically charming libertine Becka, the drily funny, straight-edged, neurotic Albert, the Thursday night movie kids and the rest—are here a lot too.

They're just the current bunch, gathered around Robby and his guitar. But, with the exception of an eighteen-month period after the birth of child number four during which we hunkered down in survival mode, there's been someone around for all our time here. A year ago it was a knot of complex, intense, brilliant, clean-cut young men considering religious vocations who came for poetry readings and complex, intense, brilliant discussions about literature and spirituality, and who were bemused when this lot started hanging around wearing bandanas and leaving cigarette butts in the bushes. Groups evolve fairly fluidly; we wait to see who turns up and adjust accordingly.

Students who find their way here do so for a variety of reasons. Some like having a place to hang out away from a campus social scene that they find dangerous or distasteful or tedious. Some are homesick and like being around domestic life and children. Some need a temporary port in a crisis. Some are intrigued by our vaguely bohemian household—homeschooling, no TV, organic yogurt—and hang around to watch in case they want to try some of it themselves someday. Some, I guess, just like us. Some run out of money, and need to be fed or housed for a while. Some use us as a sounding board for ideas they are working through. Robby, who is attempting—with rather mixed results but with sincerity—to live more thoughtfully and intentionally than in his heedless high school days, knew that we would get his reasons for skipping the teenage-girls-in-hot-tub scene, and came in search of understanding and affirmation as well as of tea and fried eggs.

I think we've been able to be of some use to some of them, though by and large we'll never know. Certainly we've learned a lot from them. One crew, years ago now, told us without a trace of irony about a priest so holy that he would levitate during mass, and was obliged to keep a tame squirrel on his shoulder during the liturgy to keep him from drifting into religious ecstasy. The lot who succeeded them advised us, with equal sincerity, that drug dealers who are themselves addicts are frequently quite nice people, whereas those who do not use are generally very dangerous and should be avoided. Robby is teaching us guitar.

They have also taught me to expand my human sympathies. My grown-up friends tend, probably inevitably, to be people quite like me. Now there's legitimate comfort in the company of one's own sort, but too much of it and one can slip into the toxic error of thinking that all the good people are people of one's own sort. Some of the students who come round here are quite like us too: Albert is precisely the sort of person I was friends with when I was in college. But my censorious, overachieving, nineteen-year-old self would have found Robby and Becka and Paul both contemptible and threatening and wanted nothing to do with them. From the majestic heights of forty-two it is easy to look over the barriers of my own petty prejudices and to appreciate and love them as they are. Foul-mouthed, chain-smoking hipsters, I have learned, are people too and sometimes deeply kind and warmhearted people.

Over the years a lot of time that could have gone into reading and writing has gone into movie nights, bonfire jam sessions, and late-night conversations earnest, frivolous, pensive, or riotous. A lot of money that could have gone into home repairs or clothes from somewhere a bit more upscale than Target has gone into mountains of spaghetti, lakes of curry, and acres of Glen's renowned apple pie. I don't regret a minute or a dollar of it: certainly we could be a good deal more productive in a number of ways if we organized ourselves differently, but I can't imagine enjoying it more. I hope that Joe and Linette had as much fun as we do. I really like having these kids in and out. I like their hilarity, their intensity, their warmth. I like the chaos, the mess, the stream of stories, the late nights, the never knowing when somebody will show up and start making cookies.

Most particularly I like that they are making themselves up as they go along. I love watching them bricolage their way out of adolescence and into adulthood, trying on and discarding self-images, life plans, loves, like Abercrombie hoodies. It keeps me honest; it reminds me that many of my own settled tastes, habits, and even convictions were doubtless picked up more or less arbitrarily in the fast-flowing tumult of my own college years, and fitted together on the fly. It helps me resist the impulse to retrofit a smug and artificial coherence to my own middle-aged self. C. S. Lewis writes that the man who learns to appreciate fine wine, but in the process loses his taste for lemonade, has in effect gained nothing; so also the woman who learns the stability and fidelity of adulthood, but in doing so learns to despise the full-hearted folly of youth.

Hospitality, in one form or another, has become the theme of my adult life. The flow of people has been the background, and often the foreground, against which my thought, and my understanding of my own life as a scholar, as a teacher, as a wife and mother, as a Christian, as a modern middle-class Westerner, have matured. My virtues, such as they are, the areas where my life is relatively sound and good, are largely connected with hospitality. My sins and failures, the bits of my life that are cold or unbalanced or ragged or wrong, are failures of those virtues. The premise of this book is that hospitality is a good thing to do, a practice worth cultivating that has something to offer our culture. The argument of this book is that it is more than that.

There is a saying; "A stranger is just a friend you haven't met yet." This is saccharine nonsense, of course, the flaccid wisdom of gift-shop mugs. A friend, even the closest friend, always to some extent remains a stranger; always a mystery, always an *other*. Each of us has an inner life that is ineluctably, inalienably private. I can, ultimately, be no one but myself, think no one's thoughts, feel no one's feelings but my own. But we are also drawn to relationship, to community with other selves, as profoundly as we are drawn to life itself, and this calls us to expand ourselves, to imagine and identify with other selves, other thoughts and feelings.

The tension between our inherent solitude and our inherent desire for union is, perhaps, a pale reflection of our creation in the image of a God who is Three and One. The mystery of the Trinitarian life is one of perfect poise—the perfect integrity, the simplicity of one Being, the perfect loving union of three Persons. We, on the other hand, are constantly off-kilter, seesawing crazily between egotism and neediness, struggling for balance, weaving around, tugging on, toppling into each other, helplessly or blindly or viciously. Every human encounter invites us to adjust our fragile equilibrium to the pull or push of a new other.

Hospitality has been for me an education, a training in balance, in self-knowledge. The central argument of this book is that hospitality can serve as a useful metaphor for other aspects of life, that the notion of welcome can be a fruitful way to think of one's relationship not only to visitors and strangers, but also to ideas, to people, to God. In the first chapter, I will explore a few examples of the sorts of things that happen when people invite other people into their homes, and use these to develop a model of genuine welcome. In subsequent chapters I will apply this model to other areas of human experience: to marriage, to the intellectual life, to spirituality. Thus, having begun with my own story, the book will move outwards, taking in other stories, to consider what exactly is going on when one welcomes people into one's space, feeds them, and listens to *their* stories, and what it can teach us.

1

The Place We Start From

Hospitality and the Home

Christian treatments of hospitality almost always begin with the story of Abraham at Mamre, told in Genesis 18. When Abraham welcomed the three men who appeared at his tent door "in the heat of the day," he welcomed God and the covenant with him. The whole glorious and awful story of salvation history blossoms from that moment of welcome.

It's not clear whether Abraham knew exactly who he was dealing with; the story, and Abraham's behavior, and what follows from it, crosses back and forth over the lines between realism and national myth. But whether Abraham at any moment is best understood as an ancestral archetype or as a real historical nomad, he would have welcomed the strangers regardless of whom he believed them to be. In desert cultures like Abraham's, a traveler's survival depended on the welcome and generosity of those he encountered, and those cultures put a correspondingly high value on hospitality; it was a matter of life and death.

The kind of precariousness and dependence that was central to the experience of travelers in the deserts of the ancient world is largely foreign to that of most people likely to read this book.

Motels and credit cards and technology and affluence and fast food restaurants and GPS gadgets and all those things that make the modern West such a bizarrely comfortable place to live in some ways (and so uncomfortably bizarre in other, less tangible ways) have gone a long way to insulating most of us from our own vulnerability and from that of others. Even if we know better, in practice most of us proceed on the assumption that feeling safe in our environment, and self-sufficient in our safety, is the normal condition of human life. We are dependent, of course, and vulnerable; deeply and awfully so. We depend, however, not on something obvious, and discrete, like the generosity of the old man in the tent under the terebinths, whom we can see clearly, and on whose immediate response to our immediate needs our life hangs, but on structures so large and complex that we can't keep them in focus at all, and can't begin to unravel the notion of what would happen if they weren't there.

Ironically, then, as our experience of vulnerability has narrowed so has our definition of the hospitality that responds to it, until for many of us it means no more than "entertaining family and friends."[1] Insofar as the encounter with a stranger is an encounter with God, as it was for Abraham, this is indeed a cripplingly narrow definition. Contemporary culture does more than cripple and constrict our notions of hospitality, however; it deforms and distorts them. What, for instance, is one to make of the phrase "hospitality *industry*"? Or of the manuals and magazines and cable shows offering advice about hospitality-as-entertaining that seem to have less to do with actually *entertaining* one's friends and family than with impressing or even intimidating them with fancy food and elaborate centerpieces?

Of course this debasement of the term does not go unchallenged. Many Christians make an eloquent case for a radical reclaiming of the Christian tradition of hospitality.[2] To practice authentic hospitality, they argue—to be truly a child of Abraham

---

1. Pohl, *Making Room*, 3.
2. Pohl's book, cited above, is an excellent example.

in his welcome of the three men at Mamre—is to be open to the reality of human vulnerability and dependence, in oneself and in those in whom it is most obvious: the poor, the marginalized, the handicapped, the refugee, the sick, the addict, the suffering. These writers are entirely right. I should do this. Of course I should do this. We should all do this. And of course there are many more people, daring, selfless people, most of them not of the book-writing sort, who *do* do this—individually and in churches from all across the spectrum, and in a myriad of communities, some of which we will look at later.

But, like most of us, I don't do this: our keeping an open house to bright middle-class kids is a small timid step towards the heights and depths of Christian hospitality. But small timid steps are all that many of us are likely to attempt or to comprehend readily. And, as Abraham's world is so alien to us, it may be helpful to begin with what is relatively familiar, with the business of "entertaining family and friends," and to see what we can learn from there about the nature of hospitality, and what the practicing of it can teach us about human life. What we do when we bring people into our homes both reveals and shapes who we are. It reveals who we are by helping us understand the extent and limits of our openness to others. It shapes us because having our lives, our spaces, our time, our routines and habits disarranged by the presence of others can disarrange our egos and challenge our instinctive sense of being at the center of things. Letting people into our kitchens and spare rooms, laying extra places, cooking extra food, washing extra dishes, staying up extra late, hearing new stories, digging out inflatable mattresses and extra towels, stretching our spaces and budgets and energy around the needs and personalities of our guests can stretch our sympathies, expand our hearts, our understandings of ourselves and of the world and our place in it.

So: three stories. They have in common the theme of people inviting others into their homes, sharing space and food and time with them. What distinguishes them is the attitudes of the hosts: to themselves, to their homes, to their guests. The first serves as a strident counter-example; how not to do it. It will stand as an emblem of what I will call an attitude of control. The second represents what I will call surrender, and functions as a cautionary tale: things to be careful of. The third story represents what I think of as genuine welcome: how hospitality can work when it really works.

The first story, from Proust's *Remembrance of Things Past*, is simple: Swann, in love with Odette, pursues her to the house of her friends the Verdurins where she spends her evenings, becomes drawn into their world as his relationship with her progresses, accidentally offends Mme. Verdurin, and is alienated from their circle.

The Verdurins have a "salon" where their regular guests, "the faithful," the "little nucleus," gather almost every evening for food, games, music and conversation. In the formal and rigidly stratified world of Parisian society it is a haven of comfort and of deliberate informality. The Verdurins are wealthy, and generous with their wealth; they feed their guests, take them to the theater, to restaurants, even on holiday. They nurture and appreciate the talents of the young painter and the pianist who are part of the "little nucleus." It is, initially, an appealing arrangement: intensely so to someone like me. The Verdurin's salon is in many ways the kind of open house space we try to create here; a place where people can show up, get away from the varied pressures of campus life, know that they are welcome and can relax. It is appealing, then, but it quickly becomes apparent that the whole setup, the expenditure of time and money and attention, is a vast contraption to feed the insatiable vanity and egoism of Mme. Verdurin. If Mme. Verdurin values her guests at all, it is only because she can exercise on them, and display before them, her own personality. The salon, its air of informality and generosity, functions only to affirm Mme. Verdurin's informality and generosity. Her appreciation of and sensitivity to art and music is not about art and music but entirely about her own appreciative and sensitive nature. Her affectionate concern for her guests is a performance of affection and concern. Mme Verdurin's personality, and her monstrous vanity, is always at the center of the salon, whose purpose is to mirror it back to her.

Vanity is among the shallower sins, and thus far Mme. Verdurin is no worse than ridiculous. Swann, an art critic and collector who is vastly more cultivated than the Verdurins and has moved in much higher society than that of the "little nucleus," manages to overlook her folly, to be devoted to her, and even to believe her "great-hearted." He effectively abandons his other circles, and spends most of his free time with Odette at the Verdurins'. But Mme. Verdurin is something rather worse than vain and ridiculous. She does not only require patience and toleration from her guests, she demands exclusive fidelity, and explicit assent to the rigid dogma that governs the salon; that the Verdurins' is the only place where one might possibly want to spend time, that "the evenings spent by other people, in other houses than theirs, were as dull as ditch-water," that the entire social world outside of the "little clan" is full of "bores."[3]

This demand leads to Swann's downfall. It never occurs to him to mention, among the little nucleus, the other world to which he has access, but neither does it occur to him, when a newcomer to the group mentions Swann's aristocratic connections, that he is required openly to disavow them as "bores." Mme. Verdurin is wounded, offended, and angered by the discovery that her drawing room does not constitute Swann's entire horizon: subtly, but swiftly and brutally, he finds himself first excluded from the "little clan" and later alienated from Odette, whom Mme. Verdurin encourages to move onto other men, whom Mme. Verdurin is better able to control.

What are we to make of Mme. Verdurin and her "hospitality?" A return to the story of the men who appear to Abraham at Mamre can help us here. When they leave Abraham they go on to the city of Sodom, where they are received by Abraham's

3. Proust, *Remembrance of Things Past,* 205.

nephew Lot (the story is in Genesis 19). In the middle of the night a posse comes to Lot's door demanding that he send his guests out to them; they want to have sex with them. Now it is a long way from gang rape in a desert city to passive-aggression in a Parisian drawing room, but in her own way Mme. Verdurin, although superficially a host like Abraham and Lot, is not unlike the men of Sodom. Like them she sees other people as objects, as tools that she can use to achieve her personal goals. Like them she is utterly indifferent to the humanity of the guests, their own stories, their lives. The men of Sodom don't care who Lot's guests are, where they come from, where they are going or why; they simply want to make use of their bodies for their own sexual plea-sure. Mme. Verdurin, likewise, has no interest in the personhood of her guests, their stories, their likes, their loves, their talents, except insofar as they can serve as arenas for her to exercise her own perceived virtues of sympathy, encouragement, generosity.

The men of Sodom are motivated by lust, Mme. Verdurin by vanity, but also by fear. At the heart of her behavior is the horror of emptiness, of her own nothingness. The accessories that she makes of her guests do not ornament her, they consti-tute her; she is utterly identified with her role as hostess, utterly dependent on her guests to sustain her in that role, outside of which she has no integrity, no authentic identity. Any hint that they might have other loyalties, other perspectives that might challenge the orthodoxy that governs the salon is so terrifying that it must be eliminated. She appears to welcome, but in real-ity she seeks only to assimilate, to control. In her own way she is as hostile and as violent as the men of Sodom.

If Mme. Verdurin is like the men of Sodom, regarding her guests as objects for her private gratification, then surely the an-swer is to turn back to the example of Abraham, whose hospital-ity the story of Sodom throws into relief. This is just what Moshe and his wife Malli do, very literally, in the Israeli film *Ushpizin*: our second story. Moshe and Malli are deeply, extravagantly faithful Hasidic Jews, living in minute obedience to the Torah, passionately devoted to God, willing to stake everything on their trust in his provision. The story unfolds during the Festival of Booths, a weeklong holiday during which observant Jews live in *sukkot*—temporary outdoor huts—in commemoration of the forty years in the wilderness. Into their *sukkah*, and into their lives, come Eliyahu and Yossef, friends of Moshe's from his past, from the days before he found his way to a religious life of strict observance. Eliyahu and Yossef have escaped from prison and are on the run. Moshe's *sukkah*, tucked away in a courtyard in an ultra-Orthodox neighborhood of Jerusalem, furnished with cots and abundant holiday food, is an excellent place to lie low. They are happy to exploit the newfound piety of their old companion, who has turned away from a life of anger and violence to one of trust, devotion, and obedience.

The transaction between the characters is more complex and subtle, however, than naked exploitation of hosts by guests. Eliyahu and Yossef serve a purpose in the lives of Moshe and Malli, who regard their guests as an answer to prayer and an opportunity to increase their own holiness by honoring the commandment to welcome guests (*ushpizin*) into the *sukkah*. As it becomes plain, first, that the guests are uncouth and dis-respectful and, later, that they are malicious and threatening, Moshe and Malli come to see them as a test, given to them by God to prove their fidelity, their readiness to be trustfully obedient to the divine will. They not only take Abraham and Sarah as religious examples, but identify personally with them: like Abraham and Sarah they are childless. When Abraham had welcomed the three men, they told him that Sarah would bear him a son.

But they miss an important point about the story in Genesis 18. Abraham goes out to meet the men, begs them to rest, to wash, to eat "that you may refresh yourselves." He further says, "and after that you may pass on." He acknowledges that they are on a journey, that they have their own story, and that after a bath, a nap, and a meal, it is appropriate that they move back into that story. Moshe and Malli's naive piety, ironically, prevents them from seeing their guests as people with their own stories. Mme. Verdurin, as we saw, views her guests as tools in her desperate attempt to fill the yawning emptiness of her own echoing ego; their individuality is a matter of complete indifference to her. Likewise, Moshe and Malli are not the least interested in Eliyahu and Yossef's motivation, their predicament, their rough charm, nor even the real menace they come to represent. Nor do the hosts attempt to set any appropriate limits to the relationship with their guests. They are willing to surrender their own comfort, and eventually their security and that of their neighbors— and even the integrity of their marriage—to God, if that is what is asked of them, but in this surrender to the divine demands of hospitality they avoid a genuine human encounter with their guests, whom they see as pawns in a transaction involving only themselves and God. Eliyahu finds Moshe's piety and all its trappings ridiculous, but is shrewdly aware that he is essentially an instrument to Moshe as Moshe is to him, and uses this awareness to justify increasingly aggressive exploitation. "He wants to be a saint," he tells Yossef, "let him practice hospitality." Moshe, for his part, is clear-eyed about his own attitude. "What are you?" he asks his guests. "You are nothing. No Yossef, no Eliyahu, nothing. There's only God."

Moshe and Malli's insistence on seeing the situation entirely as a divine and not as a human drama, and their consequent surrender to their guests' demands, their failure to put any reasonable or prudent limits on their hospitality strains their human limits to the breaking point. Malli leaves, and Moshe is driven to despair and almost to violence. Their story has the happy ending it deserves, however. Moshe and Malli's reckless goodness and love for God is rewarded: she returns, pregnant, and the film's final scene, at their son's circumcision, suggests that they have ventured into an authentic and realistic human friendship with Eliyahu and Yossef. This *deus ex machina* resolution is perfectly appropriate to a film that comes down unabashedly on the side

of grace. Most of *Ushpizin*, however, concerns the complex relationship of mutual exploitation between two worlds; that of the
guests governed by cynicism and expediency, that of the hosts by
daring and guileless faith, both unable to see beyond their own
realities to the reality of the other. However noble its motivation,
surrender, like control, can mar hospitality, make it into something other than genuinely human welcome.

What, then, does real welcome look like? Our third story
is the 1987 Danish film *Babette's Feast*, adapted from the 1958
story by Isak Dinesen. Martine and Philippa are elderly spinsters, leaders, since their father's death, of an ascetic Lutheran
sect on the Danish coast. In their youth, both had a brush with
the broader world in the form of a romance (Martine's with
a cavalry officer, Philippa's with a Parisian opera singer) that
was rejected in favor of devotion to the deeply unworldly piety
of their father's work. They dedicate themselves to their small
congregation, and to good works among the poor and sick.
Into this narrow world comes a refugee from an altogether different sphere. On a stormy night in 1872, Babette appears on
their doorstep, battered and despairing, bringing a letter from
Philippa's former suitor, the opera singer Papin, explaining her
situation. She is fleeing the war in France, in which her husband
and son had been killed; she managed to secure a place on a
ship to Denmark and had asked her Papin if he knew any "good
people" there from his travels. Papin begs the sisters to "receive
her mercifully." "Babette can cook," he concludes.[4]

The sisters are "alarmed and dismayed" by Babette: by the
strangeness and violence of her story, by "the idea of French luxury
and extravagance," and by the strain that an extra person presents
to their modest resources. But, their hearts moved by compassion

---

4. Dinesen, "Babette's Feast," 30. Quotations, for the sake of convenience,
are taken from the Dinesen text. My use of *Babette's Feast,* however, relies
more on the film version, which is, for the most part, extraordinarily faithful
to the story, but which departs from it at the end to the extent of a couple of
extremely significant omissions. Unlike Dinesen's story, Axel's film is, I believe,
profoundly Christian.

for her plight and their habits formed by a lifetime of service, they defy their anxieties and they take her in. The Frenchwoman becomes part of their world, and the sisters become as dependent on Babette as she is on them. She learns to cook their simple food, to help deftly with their charitable works, and to bargain so shrewdly in the marketplace that their small income goes further than before. In a sense it is a symbiosis as complete as that which Mme. Verdurin seeks. But although Babette is an integral part of the sisters' world, she remains fundamentally alien to it. There are deep sorrows and mysteries in her character of which Martine and Philippa are acutely aware, but which they do not try to probe; they know that "in the soundings of her being there were passions, there were memories and longings of which they knew nothing at all," and they respect the privacy of her loss.[5]

After fourteen years of this quiet existence, as the sisters are preparing to celebrate the centenary of their father's birth, and are worried by the petty personal divisions growing within their aging and increasingly crotchety flock, Babette's other, lost world becomes a reality in theirs. Her one contact with France has been an annual lottery ticket, and she has won ten thousand francs—a sum quite astonishing to the sisters. Martine and Philippa are as dismayed by this news as is Mme. Verdurin by the revelation that Swann was a regular visitor to the salons of the aristocracy.

> They realized that the happenings concerned themselves as well as Babette. The country of France, they felt, was slowly rising before their servant's horizon and correspondingly their own existence was sinking beneath their feet . . . The congratulations died on their lips, and the two pious women were ashamed of their own silence.

Unlike Mme. Verdurin, Martine and Philippa are alert to, and ashamed of, the fundamental selfishness of their own response, and are thus able to resist it. They feel no bitterness: they had

5. Ibid., 34.

never deluded themselves that they truly owned Babette, and thus can accept her departure with sorrowful equanimity. "Birds will return to their nests," they tell each other, "and human beings to the country of their birth."[6]

But as they prepare themselves to let Babette go she comes to them with a request: she wants to cook the dinner in celebration of the minister's centenary, "a real French dinner," which she insists on paying for with her own money. Martine and Philippa demur. A French dinner, with all its suggestions of excess, hedonism and decadence, is quite beyond their narrow experience, and directly opposed to the asceticism of their culture. "To them," as they had told Babette when she arrived, "luxurious fare was sinful." They are firmly opposed, moreover, to allowing their servant to spend her own money on them. Babette overpowers them, however, with an eloquent plea.

> Ladies! Had she ever, during twelve years, asked a favor? No! . . . Tonight she had a prayer to make, from the bottom of her heart. . . . The ladies for a while said nothing. Babette was right; it was her first request these twelve years.

They grant her request, and her evident joy leads them to wonder "whether in this hour they themselves had not, for the very first time, become to her the 'good people' of Achille Papin's letter."[7]

The sisters immediately find themselves plunged into an alarming world. Babette whirls into action; a shipment of mysterious and exotic goods arrives by ship from France. Martine is shocked by the wine, and downright terrified by the apparition of a live turtle. The approaching meal takes on occult dimensions in her imagination—"a witches' sabbath"—and Babette herself appears as a demon.[8] In distress she confesses to the Brotherhood the threat she has unwittingly brought upon them and the dilemma

6. Ibid, 36.
7. Ibid., 38.
8. Ibid., 40, 39.

they are now facing. The Brotherhood's alarm at the notion of be-ing forced to eat good food is the comical fruit of a doctrine and a moral life marked by cramped narrowness and lack of imagi-nation. They are also moved, however, by genuine affection for the sisters and for Babette herself, and their doctrine and life are shaped by ingrained habits of renunciation and self-discipline. The choice is clear to them; "they had never in their life broken a promise," and to do so is inconceivable, so they face the danger together, joining hands first on a solemn vow that they will rise above the sensual temptations they are facing: "On the day of our master we will cleanse our tongues of all taste and purify them of all delight and disgust of the senses, keeping and preserving them for the higher things of praise and thanksgiving."[9]

In the course of their relationship with Babette, and par-ticularly in this moment, the sisters succeed in doing what both Mme. Verdurin and Moshe and Malli failed in their different ways to do; they offer a real welcome. Unlike Mme. Verdurin they open themselves genuinely to a stranger and, with her, to a world that challenges and destabilizes the cozy certainties of their own. But they, unlike Moshe and Malli, do so without surrendering the integrity of their own world. The sisters had mercifully received Babette into a household that had a clear character of its own. Babette had never acted so as to destabilize that character, never challenged the doctrine that "their own food must be as plain as possible; it was the soup-pails and baskets for their poor that signified," but had rather accepted it, and become integral to it. It is only after twelve years of split cod and soup-pails, of growing mutual respect and trust, that the sisters "gave themselves into their cook's hands."[10]

Babette's feast is transformative. The Brotherhood, bound by their vow, tremblingly accept from Babette's hands the sinis-ter and occult mysteries of French cuisine: Clos Vougeot, Blinis Demidoff, and Cailles en Sarcophage. They are elevated and

9. Ibid., 41.
10. Ibid., 39.

warmed, by the wine and by the novel experience of sensual pleasure that they had always shunned; long-cherished hurts are forgotten, old rifts are reconciled, the faith of the community is renewed. The transformation works both ways, however. At the Paris restaurant where Babette had been head chef, she had cooked for people who appreciated the greatness of her food but who, by her own admission, were "evil and cruel." Now she prepares food for people who are trained by long habit, and committed by solemn vow, to valuing the life of the spirit over that of the flesh. The food gives them pleasure, but they give the meal meaning; the severe, ascetical righteousness of the Brotherhood transforms the amoral epicurean bliss of Babette's food into an experience that is not only physical and emotional but spiritual: "the fulfillment of an ever-present hope . . . an hour of the millennium."[11]

We will return to Babette's feast in a later chapter. For now, let us look over these three stories and see what their forms of hospitality have to teach us. Mme. Verdurin, then. Mme. Verdurin makes me shudder. In part it is a satisfying, ironical shudder of contempt and conscious superiority; I am reading the book and can see how awful she is, and she is in the book and can't. But it's more than that: it's a shudder of fear and, at bottom, of empathy. I know why she is so awful, because I could be that way too. I understand the compulsive need for attention, affirmation, and control that directs her behavior and underlies the masquerade of warm, informal hospitality. In the end, my main response to Mme. Verdurin is one of gratitude. Had I not met her before we started on this open-house business I might have become her. Had she not shown me so clearly what a toxic brew of hospitality mixed with neediness and vanity can make, I might have been inclined to cook up something similar myself. (Though I trust I wouldn't have gotten there; Glen, who has a great deal more to him than the ineffectual Mme. Verdurin and who doesn't hesitate to call me out when necessary, wouldn't have let that happen.)

11. Ibid., 54.

This, of course, is a personal reaction; there are some things about Mme. Verdurin that are altogether too familiar for comfort. But there are, I suspect, very few people who cannot to some degree relate to her compulsive self-centeredness. We all start from our own selves—our needs, our impulses, our fears—and whatever attempts we make to be good people involve an ongoing negotiation with our ego. It is in the nature of consciousness that we see our own selves as occupying the center of the universe, and other selves as revolving around us, at greater or lesser distances. But then it was quite natural too for people to assume that the earth sat still at the center of the universe and that the sun and moon orbited around it. That's what it looks like, after all. The only problem is that it's flat out wrong. It took some serious intellectual effort on the part of a handful of geniuses to figure this out, but now that they have done it we all know that we are in fact whirling through space at one hundred thousand miles an hour on a tiny speck of rock in an unbounded universe. Every one of us, however, has to figure for ourselves what to do with the equivalent truth—that we are no more important than any of the six billion people with whom we share the whirling rock, or than the billions who lived here and made human history before we arrived. We know in theory that other people's selves—their needs, their impulses, their fears—are every bit as real and as important as ours are, but truly to realize and internalize it is a lifelong journey which none of us fully completes and which some of us never really begin.

Of course there are resources to help us realize and live with this truth: cultures, religions, philosophies, communities, practices. Hospitality is one such practice, at least potentially; to share with others the little bit of physical space that we occupy, can teach us to share with them the place at the center of the universe that we are inclined to think we occupy. This is precisely what Mme. Verdurin fails to do. Far from challenging or undermining her human delusion about her own importance, her salon merely shores it up: her drawing room is not a place for human encounter but the gravity field of her ego: she demands of her guests that they be not people in their own right, but merely satellites in orbit around her. The hospitality of which she is so vain is nothing of the sort, but is rather a futile attempt to control everyone around her. She refuses to take a step away from her position at the absolute center of her world; refuses to let herself come under the gravitational influence of anybody else's personality or experience.

Once one does take that step, once one begins to grasp that other people are as real as oneself, the implications are as dizzying and as terrifying as those of Galileo's discovery, or of the incomprehensibly vast numbers in which modern physics deals. What right do I have to own hundreds of books, to have six pairs of shoes, to eat three meals a day, when there are other people, every bit as important as me, who are illiterate, barefoot, and malnourished? If it comes to that what right do I have to two kidneys or two lungs when there are people who are dying for the need of them? If the happiness and the suffering of others matters every bit as much as my own, how can I make any claims for myself? What business do I have imposing any limits on the claims others make on me? Surely I am guilty, infinitely responsible, perpetually, hopelessly indebted? As there is no corner of my self that is proof against the claims of others, then surely the only way to live is to be perpetually open to those claims: as there are no self-evident boundaries, surely one should not impose artificial, self-serving ones, but rather live without them?

This is what Moshe and Malli try to do. They want, passionately and guilelessly, to be saints, to abandon themselves to utter generosity, to break out of their own wants and fears, to throw down the cramped and stifling boundaries of the ego. But they find that they simply cannot do it: that they cannot transcend the need for basic boundaries, arbitrary or otherwise, for some defense of their own space, security, dignity, and peace of mind against the importunate claims of their guests. Their surrender to Eliyahu and Yossef is a deliberate religious act rather than a personal one, but all the same a spiritual path that almost leads to personal disaster until the human relationships are faced and resolved, and basic human needs acknowledged and met.

To stretch our astronomical metaphor a little further, Mme. Verdurin is a black hole, sucking into itself every object that comes within range of her ego. Moshe and Malli, on the other hand, abandon their own center and nearly spin out of control. Martine and Philippa, however, and the guest who becomes their host, orbit around each other, balanced and harmonious. In their relationship, a favorite passage of the old minster's is incarnate: "Mercy and Truth, dear brethren, have met together," the sisters' father used to say. "Righteousness and Bliss have kissed one another."[12]

To understand their case better we can move from a metaphor drawn from science to one of art. "I am a great artist," Babette tells the sisters after the meal. Her hosts, in their own way, are also artists. It is the art of the chef to balance ingredients, flavors, textures so that they complement and enhance each other, and the art of the host to negotiate between the needs of the self and those of the other, between the claims and gifts of the home and its inhabitants and those of the guest, until a balance is reached in which both are enriched. With the advent of Babette, Martine and Philippa find themselves caught in the pull between two imperatives that are equally crucial ingredients in the pattern of their lives and their sense of self and that have, until now, been easily harmonious: on the one hand, simplicity and asceticism, on the other, charity to the needy and the refugee. In the sisters' place, a Mme. Verdurin would have taken Babette in as a conquest, would have proselytized and bullied and patronized out of her any traces of allegiance to a world different from that of her hostess, glorying in her own control and the refugee's dependence. Moshe and Malli would have retreated into neutral generosity before her, would have refused to assert themselves, to make any demands on her, and in so doing would have retreated from authentic relationship with her. The sisters do neither. They

12. Ibid., 24–25.

allow Babette her privacy, but they also allow themselves their integrity and comfort. They respect her strangeness, but they also respect their own traditions. They expect her to learn to live in a way that is harmonious with their beliefs, but they do not expect her to share them. And in so doing they build and sustain a relationship of genuine human affection, trust, and respect with the alien in their midst, which allows them to respond to the challenge she presents. They travel out from themselves and come back transformed, never realizing, in their humility, that as they are elevated by the artistry of her food, they are also "exalted by their own merit."[13]

As Mme. Verdurin, then, will serve us as a model of hospitality twisted by egotism into control, and Moshe and Malli of hospitality threatened by imprudent surrender and a lack of discerning wisdom, so Martine and Philippa will be our examples of genuine welcome. A good host, I contend, is one who welcomes the guest into a home that has a definite character, and does so in such as way that the guest's personality becomes an authentic part of that character.

This, in a very homely, very dusty idiom, is what I found at Joe and Linette's. Their house was an entirely distinctive space. Their personalities, their eccentricities, their likes and dislikes and tastes and habits were written all over it. And their personalities were strong and clear; in welcoming all comers they made no surrender of their own individuality. Nor did they ask that we surrender ours; there was no attempt to control, to manipulate or bully visitors into conforming to the house style. They simply provided a place where we could show up with our toothbrushes, notes, questions, friends, and worries: speak frankly, act freely, be well fed and well listened to, with intelligent interest but without intrusive curiosity, and be sent back into our own world with an open invitation to return. This kind of welcome, one which honors the integrity of both host and guest and creates a space where they can come together, is what we try to practice, and what I will attempt to explore here.

13. Ibid., 53.

2

Adoring Her Husband's Virtues

Hospitality and the Heart

As Babette's feast approaches, Martine has a nightmare in which Babette poisons all of the Brotherhood. I know how she felt: I've had one of those too. When I was in grad school, courting Glen (a wildly archaic term but better suited for what was going on than "dating"), I had a little white room in a basement apartment, with a little white bed and a big white desk. Very monastic, very demure, very virginal. One night I dreamt that Glen arrived with a team of strangers and was trying to move furniture into my demure, virginal little room: paintings, ornaments, overstuffed armchairs, and a vast, ornately carved, Tudor four-poster bed. I was furious and terrified. I screamed at them, tried to beat them back, to force the door against them; by my (admittedly rather tame) standards it was a very violent dream. I woke up sweating and agitated, collected myself, and then laughed. I'm no Freudian analyst, but this one was too glaringly obvious—an image of my poor little psyche shrinking from the invasion of another person in his totality.

The inner panic that expressed itself in my dream is comical, to be sure, but it wasn't, perhaps, altogether unreasonable. The person who catches your eye and tugs at your heart and fills up your thoughts is like the person who appears at your tent door in the heat of the day—a stranger full of unknown threat and promise, who has the potential to be anything and to change everything. You invite him for coffee, he invites you for dinner, you invite him to your cousin's wedding, he invites you to his parents' for Thanksgiving, you invite him to hear your stories, he invites you to understand his anxieties . . . you invite each other into bed and board and bank account, better and worse and sickness and health and happily ever after. Many stories—novels, plays, movies—end here, with the couple finally united, in expectation of a stable, loving, and harmonious union, the focus of many of the hopes for happiness of much of the human race. But lives, unlike novels, rarely end with the orange-blossom bliss of weddings, and what follows the vows leaves no area of life untouched, unchanged, untampered with. When you are bound together with someone in the till-death-do-us-part union of marriage, not only personal space, but also everything else—privacy, independence, solitude, money, religion, political allegiance—are all in the mix; even the body itself is open to the other.

Marriage is thus the arena for a particularly intense form of hospitality. And it is two-sided. Both of you have to be simultaneously guest and host; it is your job both to allow another person into every corner of your own space and to make yourself at home within their space. It's a difficult business, and I give my subconscious full credit for recognizing and recoiling from the massive disruption that marriage threatens.

It is hard, and there are a hundred ways that marriages can be unhappy. Some of these are marked in garish colors: infidelity and abuse and abandonment. But many are of a subtler hue; to return to the paradigm of the last chapter, there are endless variations of control and surrender possible in marriages that are untouched by colorful drama. Three more stories, then: this time, conveniently, all from the same novel, George Eliot's 1872 *Middlemarch*, which is (also conveniently) my favorite book. I stumbled across it when I was about fourteen: I read its eight hundred or so pages in a week, turned right back to the first page and read it again. Of course there was a great deal I didn't understand, but I could tell that there was wisdom in there that I would need one day. I read it a third time, soaking in and storing up for that day. I have always gone to literature for moral education, for insight into human motivations and temptations and interactions (by necessity in my teens, as I hadn't quite mastered the knack of talking to other human beings). In the last quarter century I have sucked down a quite absurd number of novels, but this one is still an anchor for me—I go back every few years, to get my bearings.

Middlemarch is set in an English provincial town in the 1830s and tells a number of interwoven stories involving characters from a broad range of social classes. The plot is far too complex to summarize here. What concerns us are the stories of three marriages: those of Rosamund and Lydgate, Dorothea and Mr. Casaubon, and the Garths. Lydgate is a newcomer to town, a gifted, idealistic doctor with aristocratic connections but without much money, who has come to Middlemarch in the hope that he will find there more freedom than he would in London of putting into practice his experimental and reforming ideas. Welcomed into the town's professional houses, he meets Rosamund, the prettiest and most accomplished of Middlemarch's young women. He is enchanted: "She is grace itself," he tells himself. "That is what a woman ought to be: she ought to produce the effect of exquisite music."[1] Lydgate has, the narrator drily tells us, brought "a much more testing vision of details and relations into [his] pathological study than he had ever thought it necessary to apply to the complexities of love and marriage."[2] He tranquilly assumes that Rosamund's inner self will be as decorous and as decorative as her perfect blonde elegance, and that when he has married her he will have acquired for himself the devotion of "an accomplished creature who venerated his high musings and momentous labors

1. Eliot, *Middlemarch*, 84.
2. Ibid., 149.

and would never interfere with them."[3] Rosamund, for her part, had set her sights on Lydgate even before she met him, weaving him into a "preconceived romance" that would lift her out of the drab tedium of the Middlemarch bourgeoisie into a sphere more suited to her charms.[4] Their relationship progresses quickly, each constructing a fantasy in which the other supplies all of their private needs and desires and taking the thrill of these fantasies for mutual love.

"Each lived in a world of which the other knew nothing," the narrator tells us.[5] They enter marriage equally ignorant of each other and equally consumed with their own vanity: we can hold them equally to blame for what happens. But it quickly becomes clear that they are not equal in strength. Where Lydgate had fancied he would find "such help as our thoughts get from the summer sky and the flower-fringed meadow," he finds instead an inflexible egoism and "terrible tenacity" in service of a very simple goal.[6] For Rosamund, "what she liked to do was to her the right thing and all her cleverness was directed to getting the means of doing it" with no thought for the consequences.[7] Rosamund's taste for elegant living and Lydgate's haughty indifference to money get them into debt. When Lydgate tries to make her understand that they are living beyond their income and must economize, not only does she refuse to cooperate, but she also does not hesitate to sneak and betray and frustrate him. Lydgate is reduced to watching in dismay as she unhesitatingly sacrifices whatever small beginnings of trust and affection and intimacy there might have been in their marriage on the altar of her own will.

Our second *Middlemarch* marriage is a very different affair. At one level it looks much less promising than the match

3. Ibid., 320.
4. Ibid., 151.
5. Ibid., 150.
6. Ibid., 533.
7. Ibid., 532.

between the young and attractive Rosamund and Lydgate. Dorothea Brooke is an ardent, idealistic, devoutly religious young woman, Mr. Casaubon is a dry, sickly scholar and clergyman more than twice her age. Her family, friends, and neighbors all disapprove intensely of her choice on these grounds. From another point of view, however, the unconventional pairing appears suitable; unlike Rosamund and Lydgate, caught up in their private desires and delusions, Dorothea and Mr. Casaubon are explicit about their motivations for and understandings of marriage, which, although complex and idiosyncratic, do seem to complement each other.

Casaubon, like Lydgate, expects to find in marriage the support, admiration, and affection of a weaker being who will look up to him. He praises Dorothea's "elevation of thought and a capability for devotedness" and asserts that "the great charm of your sex is its capability of an ardent self-sacrificing affection, and herein we see its fitness to round and complete the existence of our own."[8] Unlike Lydgate, Casaubon has correctly perceived the main note of his fiancée's character. Dorothea shares in Casaubon's vision of their shared future. Her ideas about marriage "took their color entirely from an exalted enthusiasm about the ends of life . . . the union which attracted her was one that . . . would give her the freedom of voluntary submission to a guide who would take her along the grandest path."[9] She sees in the marriage an outlet for her intellectual and spiritual aspirations. As the helpmeet of Casaubon, whom she perceives to have a great mind and a great soul, she will be freed from the suffocating pettiness of the genteel young ladyhood that forms the entirety of Rosamund's world, will be enabled to "live continually in the light of a mind that she could reverence" and to fulfill her burning desire to do good by devotedly assisting him with his masterpiece, the *Key to All Mythologies*.[10]

8. Ibid., 37, 43.
9. Ibid., 22–23.
10. Ibid., 38.

In this case, it is Dorothea who learns that she has been sadly deluded by her naïveté, as was Lydgate by his vanity. Within a few months of their marriage Dorothea had "felt, with a stifling depression that the large vistas and wide fresh air which she had dreamt of finding in her husband's mind were replaced by ante-rooms and winding passages which seemed to lead nowhither."[11] She comes to see that Casaubon has no true vision; his intellectual life is a labyrinth of fussy pedantries. And he is no more great in soul than he is in mind. His emotional life is stunted and embit-tered by the secret awareness of his own inadequacies and by the growing certainty that his great *Key* will never be more than an inchoate mass of erudite notes on minutiae.

Dorothea's life is one of frustration on all fronts (sexual as well as intellectual and emotional: it is not something that Victorian novelists could come out and talk about, but it is clear to readers who know what clues to look for that the marriage is never consummated) and is acutely painful to her. She gradu-ally comes to perceive not only Casaubon's limitations, but also his suffering, and she struggles to find in tolerance and "a pity-ing tenderness fed by the realities of his lot and not by her own dreams" a new, muted outlet for the "active wifely devotion" she had hoped to pour into high and learned endeavors.[12] She reaches beyond her own suffering to compassion, and to the resignation that tenderness and forbearance, rather than the *Key*, must be the great work of her life.

Dorothea's course of selfless devotion is brought to a crisis by a sudden request of her husband's: "that you will let me know," he says, "whether, in case of my death, you will carry out my wishes: whether you will avoid doing what I should deprecate, and apply yourself to do what I should desire."[13] She senses im-mediately that he will want her to carry on his work on the *Key*. The grasp for control is so vicious that Dorothea, disciplined as

11. Ibid., 179.
12. Ibid., 192, 249.
13. Ibid., 435.

she has become to repressing her own needs out of pity, balks and asks for time to think. After a painful night, she finds that she cannot bear to inflict pain by refusing him: "if she were to say 'No! if you die I will put no finger to your work'—it seemed as if she would be crushing that bruised heart."[14]

Dorothea's personal character and dreams are high-minded, generous, and naive, Rosamund's petty and venal, Casaubon's grounded in self-regard and vanity, Lydgate's in vanity, idealism, and sexual desire. But they have this much in common: their desires are all private affairs of their own, which predate the relationships, and they all enter marriage not so much welcoming their partner as annexing them hopefully to the cause of their personal fulfillment. To some extent it is inevitable that they should do so. "We are all of us born in moral stupidity," Eliot says, "taking the world as an udder to feed our supreme selves," and our selves, even to the extent that they emerge from the stupidity of selfishness, remain *our* selves.[15] But a fulfilled adult life must grow beyond this instinctive egotism, must learn that the self is not supreme, that the world is not an udder for our blind desires, and that people are not things to be used.

Mme. Verdurin never learns this; nor do Casaubon and Rosamund. Neither of them grows beyond the state of moral stupidity where their primary, indeed their only, desire is to have their own way. When it becomes apparent to Casaubon that Dorothea is not going to provide the unconditional affirmation that he thought she would supply, he cannot look beyond his craving for it and see the woman to whom he has joined himself. He thought of "annexing happiness with a lovely young bride" but soon comes to see Dorothea as "a personification of that shallow world which surrounds the ill-appreciated or desponding author."[16] Much the same is true of Rosamund. When Lydgate breaks to her the news about their financial troubles, she makes

14. Ibid., 437.
15. Ibid., 249.
16. Ibid., 225, 184.

no attempt to look beyond the threat it poses to her own wants. She had looked to Lydgate to provide the elegant life she wanted; when he fails, she does not see him as a fellow victim, as a partner, as a person, but as an obstacle to goals whose legitimacy she never questions. She "no more identified herself with him than if they had been creatures of different species and opposing interests."[17]

Both Casaubon and Rosamund are, of course, unhappy. And, of course, they blame their spouses, but the fault lies with their own inability to move beyond the borders of their own egos. "Rosamund's discontent in her marriage," Eliot tells us, "was due to the conditions of marriage itself, to its demand for self-suppression and tolerance," and of Casaubon she writes that he is "under a new depression in the consciousness that the new bliss was not blissful to him."[18] Eliot has sympathy for them both, precisely because their misery is due to their human failings. She calls Rosamund a "poor thing" who "saw only that the world was not ordered to her liking" and says of Casaubon, "For my part I feel very sorry for him. It is an uneasy lot at best . . . to be present at this great spectacle of life and never to be liberated from a small, hungry, shivering self."[19] An uneasy lot indeed; in marriage, the struggle to keep the personhood of one's spouse at bay, to resist its encroachments on the imagined sovereignty of the small hungry shivering self, is terrible and exhausting. Everywhere one turns, there he is; money, food, free time, home repairs, social life—nothing is safe, nothing is fully under one's control.

Probably the main reason why I turned back to the first page of *Middlemarch* as soon as I finished the last one, and started over again was Rosamund. Although at fourteen I was naive, religious, and idealistic, I never identified with the naive, religious, idealistic Dorothea. It was Rosamund who seized me. I had an acute sense that if I wasn't careful I would become her; relentlessly self-involved, self-deceived, self-justifying, *self*-ish in all senses.

17. Ibid., 544.
18. Ibid., 689, 255.
19. Ibid., 592, 255.

It clearly was very important that I didn't do so, and I would read the book as many times as it took for me to figure out what made her that way, and how I could avoid it.

There was a while when it was a near miss. When Glen and I met, we were seriously attached to other people. Jack was in North Carolina, Samantha was in Iowa, and Glen and I were in Virginia. We rapidly became good, entirely platonic friends, with that particular easiness that is possible when one's romantic emotions are contentedly planted elsewhere and there is none of that "so, what's *really* going on here?" stuff to worry about. Then Glen went back home for a year and while he was gone I broke up with Jack, rather abruptly and for reasons I couldn't really articulate to myself at the time. Around the same time, Glen broke up with Samantha, and when it transpired that we were both single, and that he was coming back to town, things moved rather fast.

They moved fast, but much less smoothly than either of us had anticipated. Lots of clashes, lots of struggles, even fights, which neither of us had ever had with Jack and Samantha, or indeed with anybody. Had we not been such good friends before, had we not known how closely our visions meshed on the big stuff, we wouldn't have made it. As it was we were both bewildered until, as the sun rose at the end of one marathon argument, it dawned on us that we had never had this trouble in our previous relationships quite simply because we each had our own way all the time. Samantha was younger than Glen and he had always taken the lead. Jack was an extraordinarily nice chap with a deep dislike of conflict, which he dealt with by the simple expedient of never letting it arise. He wasn't a wuss; he was a person of sense and character, and I blithely considered myself fairly easygoing, so it had never occurred to me—until I found myself matched with someone of equally strong will, equally accustomed to getting his own way—that Jack had let me push him around shockingly and that I had, in fact, been well on my way to becoming Rosamund. Of course when I dreamed that Glen was trying to install awkward cumbersome pieces of furniture into my tidy, self-contained room, it wasn't really furniture that I was freaked out about at all—it was the knowledge that my world would get bigger and could no longer be ordered exclusively to my own narrow liking.

This was eighteen years ago. But Rosamund still makes me shudder, in much the same way that her older sister Mme. Verdurin makes me shudder. I still very much like getting my own way, and when I don't pay attention, I easily slide into assuming, like Rosamund, that the way I want things is simply the way they ought to be, that everyone else, most particularly Glen, should understand that and get with the program, and that if they don't then I am entirely within my rights to withdraw or sulk or whine or snap. It's no fun; it is, as Eliot says, "an uneasy lot" to be stuck with the small shivering hungry self of my inner Rosamund. But though she is alive and kicking, with the help of God and George Eliot and Glen, all of whom I can trust to call me out when necessary, she won't win.

So what are the alternatives to the tyranny of the ego, which makes love and intimacy impossible for Casaubon and Rosamund, turning marriage into a struggle for control rather than the welcome of another person into one's life? Eliot offers Lydgate and Dorothea as contrasts to their impenetrably selfish spouses. They, too, enter marriage as a means to the fulfillment of personal desires; they, too, have faults and blindness that contribute to the troubles. But Dorothea and Lydgate have emerged to a degree from the moral stupidity into which we are all born. They are better, more mature, more self-aware, more generous, larger people than their spouses. Unlike their spouses they are willing to adapt, to compromise, to abandon some of their private desires in the name of love and intimacy and unity and warmth.

Lydgate tries, clumsily but sincerely, to make their financial troubles an occasion for cooperation rather than an arena for conflict. When that fails, he assumes that he will in the nature of things win the conflict. At the time of his marriage, "Lydgate relied much on the psychological difference between what for the sake of variety I will call goose and gander; especially on the innate submissiveness of the goose as beautifully corresponding to the strength of the gander."[20] But here he proves entirely mistaken: Rosamund's "feminine impassibility" and "silvery neutrality" are impermeable to any degree of force that he is prepared to use.[21] He understands her limitations, sympathizes with her plight, and tries to resist his own anger, but can only do so at the cost of intimacy and even of the most basic fellowship. "It was inevitable that in that excusing mood he should think of her as an animal of another and feebler species," Eliot writes.[22] He finds himself powerless, "accept[s] his narrowed lot with sad resignation," and is forced to admit that "she had mastered him."[23] Unable to win or compel her understanding and cooperation, or to live with her dissatisfaction, he is forced to submit to Rosamund's control. He compromises his integrity, abandons his professional aspirations, leaves Middlemarch for London, establishes a successful practice among the wealthy and dies young, bitter, and defeated.

Lydgate is merely defeated, but Dorothea makes an attempt at a principled surrender. Like Moshe and Malli she is inspired by a lofty religious vision, and she has a richer moral imagination than Lydgate. Where he can only excuse his wife by thinking of her as "an animal of another and feebler species," she comes truly to understand that Casaubon is a fellow human, with an "equivalent center of self, whence the lights and shadows must always fall with a certain difference."[24] Dorothea's compassionate vision, as we saw, leads her to the point of explicitly pledging her entire future to her husband's wishes rather than "crushing that bruised heart." After her long night of struggle she seeks out her husband to make her promise, but before she can sacrifice herself utterly to compassion, the novelist intervenes and she finds him dead.

20. Ibid., 324.
21. Ibid., 539–40.
22. Ibid., 610.
23. Ibid.
24. Ibid., 192.

Eliot steps in to save Dorothea from a surrender of self that would have been as disastrous as Casaubon and Rosamund's selfish grasping for control. Resignation and defeat like Lydgate's is inevitably embittering, and while Dorothea's open-eyed, self-annihilating surrender to her husband's desires at the expense of her own may be admirable and spiritually powerful, it does not have the power to make a happy marriage. Their experience, like Moshe and Malli's, illustrates the other side of the problem that marriage presents and that *Middlemarch* explores. While it is true that nobody can be happy in marriage by using their spouse as a means to their private end, it is also true that each person does have an inner life, with visions, desires, and fears, a life that is inalienably their own. It can be defeated, it can be repressed, but the human desire for happiness cannot be destroyed without the destruction of humanity itself. This becomes truer as relationships get closer. Greed and dishonesty in the corridors of power rankle, but not as sharply as that of one's immediate colleagues, and while one can decide, for the sake of a quiet life, to give way to bullying or manipulative people with whom one simply doesn't have the energy to tangle, it is all but impossible to maintain one's peace of mind when the bullying or manipulation involves the intimate details of one's everyday life and the person on whom one once, however naively, had pinned one's hopes for happiness. Lydgate and Dorothea learn this painfully.

How is marriage, then, to negotiate the irreducibility of the self? How can one maintain one's own integrity and at the same time live in real intimacy with another person? How is it possible to achieve harmony with another person who has an "equivalent center of self, whence the lights and shadows must always fall with a certain difference"? How is one to welcome one's spouse and all his or her furniture into one's private room, and allow it to be changed into a new space, without finding it unrecognizable, and no longer home? In looking at the simpler business of hospitality to a guest, we found a model of genuine welcome in the story of Babette and the sisters. The secret to their relationship, we found, was in balance; Babette and the sisters managed the tension inherent between the needs of the guest and the needs of the host as a creative, graced poise, which allowed each to be host and guest to the other, each to take the risk of openness to a different world, and each to remain inalienably herself, while at the same time being profoundly transformed. Is the same true of marriage? Is it all about balance? Is the happy couple the one that has learned together the delicate art of compromise, of a relatively steady oscillation of control and surrender on both sides?

Unlike in the last chapter, where we had to jump from Paris to Jerusalem to a Norwegian fishing village to find our models, we can look for an answer to this question without having to leave the neighborhood of Middlemarch. (That's just how good the book is.) Eliot offers a pattern of a successful marriage in the persons of Caleb and Susan Garth, who, by the time we meet them, have a long-established marriage and six children, the oldest, Mary, in her twenties. Mr. and Mrs. Garth serve a crucial role as the counterpoint to the struggling unions of the younger protagonists but they are, mercifully, by no means neutral or sweetly idealized characters, like those kinds of people one meets occasionally who tell you they have a perfect marriage—"twenty-four years together and never an angry word"—and whom, I must confess, I am nastily inclined to dislike or distrust. Both have clear centers of self, where the lights and shadows fall with sharply marked individuality. He has a deep and simple nobility, but is dreamily and dangerously impractical; she is eccentric, opinionated, and sharp-tongued. Moreover, they do not have an easy time of it: Eliot hands them a series of challenges that would threaten to destabilize many a marriage.

Rosamund's brother Fred has got himself into debt and asks Caleb to co-sign a loan, assuring him breezily that he will be able to repay in time. "A large amount of painful experience," Eliot tells us, "had not sufficed to make Caleb Garth cautious about his own affairs, or distrustful of his fellow men when they had not proven themselves untrustworthy."[25] He signs the moneylender's note, and Fred's scheme to raise the money fails drastically, leaving the Garths responsible for a bill that will clean out their savings, and force Mary to go out to work and a son to abandon his education.

The disaster is averted when Caleb is asked to manage two important estates, at a good salary. But a severer trial of Mrs. Garth's devotion awaits; Caleb announces that he is going to hire Fred as his assistant. His wife is bitterly opposed. Fred has clearly proven himself to be untrustworthy, feckless, and spoiled and is likely to be a liability and a burden. Moreover, Fred has been devoted to Mary since childhood, but she has made it clear that although she loves him, she will never marry him unless he sets himself to a useful and honorable profession. If, with Caleb's help, Fred does actually get his act together, there is a good chance that Mary will marry him, and Mrs. Garth thinks his character well below her daughter. (She's right. Fred is adorable but Mary is fantastic. When I first read *Middlemarch*, my first thought was, "I must not be Rosamund Vincy," and my second was, "I have to be Mary Garth." I was ten years younger than her and at the time it didn't seem an unreasonable ambition.)

In a situation like this, where her immediate goal was different from her husband's, Rosamund would unhesitatingly have done whatever she thought was likely to get her way. And Mrs. Garth has sound cause to know that her judgment in these matters is objectively superior to her husband's. Yet having spoken her mind once, she does nothing to stop him. Has she, like Lydgate, learned over the years "sad resignation" to the inevitability of defeat? Or is she, like Dorothea, heroically and blindly surrendering: sacrificing her own peace of mind, her family's well-being, and her daughter's happiness to her husband's generous but foolish whim and her own firmly held ideology about female submission? Eliot makes clear that the relationship between the two centers of self in the Garth marriage is far more complex

25. Ibid., 210.

and nuanced than either of these possibilities, even when their lights and shadows fall at such sharply different angles as here. It is part of Mrs. Garth's shrewd realism that she possesses "that rare sense that discerns what is unalterable and submits to it without murmuring."[26] "With regard to a large number of matters about which other men are decided or obstinate," Eliot tells us of Mr. Garth:

> . . . he was the most easily manageable man in the world. He never knew what meat he would choose and if Susan had said that they ought to live in a four-roomed cottage, in order to save, he would have said, "Let us go" without inquiring into details. But where Caleb's feeling and judgment strongly pronounced, he was a ruler. . . . On ninety-nine points Mrs. Garth decided, but on the hundredth she was often aware that she would have to perform the singularly difficult task of carrying out her own principle, and to make herself subordinate.[27]

A comparison to *Babette's Feast* suggests itself here. Mrs. Garth's practical sense, like Martine and Phillipa's ascetic piety, determines the basic pattern of life in the household, and here Mr. Garth, like Babette, acquiesces without complaint. But, like Martine and Philippa, Mrs. Garth understands that there are deeper forces at work in her quiet husband, and that there are moments when, whatever the cost to her own peace of mind, she has to put her own sense and instinct to one side and trust herself to him. To this extent the Garth marriage is indeed a matter of a careful and deliberate equilibrium based on experience and mutual understanding.

This is a good thing—a very good thing—and is certainly responsible to a large degree for the fundamental harmony of the Garth household even in times of stress. But it is not all there is to the marriage; it has its roots in something deeper. In explanation of how Mrs. Garth can serenely accept those

26. Ibid., 220.
27. Ibid., 512–13.

qualities of her husband that are most frustrating to herself, Eliot says, "Adoring her husband's virtues, she had very early made up her mind to his incapacity of minding his own interests, and had met the consequences cheerfully."[28] The key word here is "virtues." Mrs. Garth adores not the qualities that are most convenient to her private vision of happiness (the aristocratic connections that Rosamund adores in Lydgate, the learning that Dorothea adores in Casaubon), but his virtues, his steadfast commitment to the good, which has carved deep, and sometimes uncomfortable, grooves in his character. Mr. Garth himself is well aware that his wife has sacrificed a great deal of comfort and security in marrying him, but when he cautions Mary about Fred, he touches on the same theme. "What it must be for a wife," he says, "when she's never sure of her husband: when he hasn't got a principle in him to make him more afraid of doing the wrong thing by others than of getting his own toes pinched."[29] It is this, what Pope John Paul II called a "union in a common true good"[30]—not one's own private good, but a good greater than oneself, well outside one's sphere of control and indeed liable to pinch one's toes—that makes good marriages between imperfect people possible. Mr. and Mrs. Garth surrender, together, to a good they have both embraced together.

What does it mean to love the good? The final good, the source and end and sum of all goods, is God. In the end, nothing but goodness itself can shame our blustering competitive egos into silence and lure our "small shivering hungry" selves out of their dens and into the light. Ultimately, the only way we can love each other—even our spouses—is if we love God first and best. But most of us, honestly, would probably slam the door and hide under the bed if goodness came in person to claim us. Most of us, even if we genuinely desire goodness, are thoroughly frightened of it and what it would demand of us, and have to grope our way

28. Ibid., 220.
29. Ibid., 234.
30. Wojtyla, *Love and Responsibility*, 163.

to faithful love and true welcome through a thicket of our own fears and greeds and meannesses. Who knows, Abraham himself might have pretended to be out if he'd really known who was coming into his life. But God, in his mercy, appeared to Abraham in the form of three strangers in the desert, and Abraham knew how to welcome strangers. Reviving grace bursts into the lives of the Brotherhood in the form of a refugee, and they follow the deep grooves that years of virtuous habit have carved into their characters when they open themselves to Babette: "They had never in their life broken a promise." And precisely where the potential for personal conflict is the sharpest, the Garths are drawn beyond themselves. "That young man's soul is in my hand," Caleb says, "and I'll do the best for him I can, so help me God! It's my duty, Susan," and Mrs. Garth, although inwardly "rational and unhopeful" about the outcome, "rose, and kissed him, saying, 'God bless you, Caleb! Our children have a good father.'"[31] As they are drawn beyond themselves they are drawn together; they push past their private wishes and into a union, a harmony, a love that is deeper than that of merely getting on, or agreeing. In welcoming Fred they welcome God, and they welcome each other.

Now that I have given up on being Mary Garth, I have set my sights on her mother as my role model. I want to be her as ardently as I want not to be Rosamund or Mme. Verdurin. I have few delusions on this score—I don't have her generosity, her resolution, her forbearance, her serenity. But I can venture one, small point of contact between the Garth and Johnson marriages. Mr. and Mrs. Garth, in welcoming the loveable but disruptive Fred, welcome God, and in welcoming God welcome each other, and Glen and I have often welcomed each other best when we have welcomed the disruptive but loveable Robby, Pat, Paul, Lara and Gabe, Eli, Franny, and the rest. The process of learning hospitality together (I wonder if the same was true for Joe and Linette) has for us been a school of marriage. We've learned to make room for each other in part by making room for other people. Many

31. Ibid., 514.

an evening in our house has begun tense and snappy because the lights and shadows of our separate selves are falling at particularly awkward angles to each other, and has ended harmoniously because others show up and hang around half the night and when they leave we turn to each other with a conspiratorial grin, or an admiring nod, or a fond chuckle, or an anxious frown, and by the time we've got the tea tray loaded and started to contemplate the wreck of the kitchen, we've forgotten whatever unimportant nonsense we were pissy about earlier because we are involved, together, in the far more interesting business of contemplating the lives and stories that the evening sent our way.

"Goodness me, she's terrific isn't she?"
"And she's not the least stuck on herself."
"Yeah, but Blaise is—had you noticed?"
"You think so? Yeah, I'd been wondering about that. Think it'll take?"

Or

"Holy crap."
"Yup."
"Poor lad means no harm, but oh dear."
"We're going to have to have a word with him, aren't we?"
"I'm afraid so. You or me?"
"Well I don't mind doing it, but I think he'd take it better from you."
"Damn. You're probably right. OK."

Or just

"Can you believe it's three in the morning?"
"Why do we let them do this to us?"
"Oh come on, it was fun. Isn't Jeremy hilarious when he gets over being shy?"
"Yeah, it was. And he is. But it's late and every mug in the house is dirty. Why do we do it to ourselves, then?"
"Oh I don't know. Come on, I'm about to fall over. Leave the dishes. Bed."

We squabble over the usual things that married people do—money, time, chores, all that stuff—but we invariably and effortlessly agree about people: one of the virtues I love most in Glen is his wisdom, both deep and incisive, about human character and motivation. So, eighteen years and counting since my subconscious freaked out at the prospect of invasion by Glen and his huge, cumbersome furniture, we're here. Sometimes, truth be told, I get frustrated at stepping around some bits of it, and wish I could rearrange and redecorate his personality and the patterns of our life together entirely to suit my tastes. I'm sure Glen feels the same. But I know—in part thanks to regular visits to Middlemarch—that even if I could, it wouldn't work, and if I ever thought it was working, that would be evidence that I was, after all, becoming Rosamund and, after all, one of the reasons I married Glen was that I could trust him to keep me from becoming Rosamund. And in the end we have proved to need all the furniture (real and metaphorical) that we can get our hands on because it is always full of people.

3

The Whole Benefit of Reading

Hospitality and the Mind

In this chapter I will suggest that ideas, as well as people, can arrive at the doors, bringing with them divine possibilities and challenges, and that welcoming them, like welcoming guests or spouses, requires that we learn to maintain a delicate balance between compulsive control and helpless surrender.

The year I met Joe and Linette I was in upheaval—joyful and terrifying at once. I had grown up in a thoroughly secular family. In the throes of puberty I had stumbled across the Christian Union at my school, and my teenage years were awash with Bible studies and prayer meetings and evangelistic events and altar calls. There are worse things that one's teenage years might be awash with; indeed I can't easily imagine a better place to sit out the normal discomforts of adolescence than among people who were largely liberated from the tiresome self-absorption of those years by the discovery that something other than themselves was at the center of the universe. It was, in some ways, my first experience of genuine welcome. I attached myself to these new friends, learned their songs, learned my way around the Good News Bible, learned their language, made it my own, made a profession of faith (a few of them, actually—it was something of a hobby for a while), was baptized wearing a long white dress with lead pellets sewn into the hem, and made earnest and occasionally tearful attempts to convert my parents, who had the good sense to listen calmly and be glad that their brainy nerd of a daughter finally had a social life.

When I got to Oxford I quickly made my home in the college Christian Union, whose friendships were at the heart of my Oxford experience. The Union part was wonderful; there were marvelous, interminable conversations, deep kindness and affection, plenty of silly exuberant fun, and a well-oiled support system. The Christian part was more of a problem. The prevalent theology of the CU was conservative evangelical with heavy emphases on personal evangelism and biblical inerrancy. It was pretty much what I had picked up in school, but there it had never been the focus; we were just trying to help each other make it to eighteen intact, and I honestly hadn't paid a great deal of attention. Here I was surrounded by clever, articulate, argumentative, and very young people firing on all cylinders, all the time, and there was constant exuberant, sometimes heated, theological debate, over a fairly narrow turf. Increasingly I began to notice it grating and pinching.

My discomfort came from a number of sources, and I tried to ignore it as much as possible, because I was having a wonderful time and I didn't want to spoil it with a crisis of faith. One of the problems was that although we talked and talked about religious subjects endlessly and vigorously, we rarely actually talked about God. We talked about doctrine and truth and Scripture and mission and evangelism and salvation and atonement, but God somehow got lost in the mix, and when I glimpsed him through the interstices of our tight-knit systems, the impression he made was such that I began to wonder whether it might not be better if humans were actually at the center of the universe after all.

It was possibly because of this void that the tightness of our systems and the firmness of our belief assumed an extraordinary importance. I felt great pressure to believe all the right things, in the right order, all the time and to move swiftly to contain and neutralize any questions or uncertainties, let alone doubts. I had a lot of doubts and they were very unnerving because, as we constantly reminded each other, we were saved by faith alone, and the badge of our salvation was an experience called "assurance" that nobody could ever quite describe to me but that I was pretty sure I didn't have. And if I didn't have assurance then I wasn't saved, but what if that wasn't true in the first place, well then where did that leave me, and so on round and round in tight, anxious circles.

In part because it provided a welcome distraction from this sort of thing, I cultivated a lively interest in people who were wrong. Non-Christians, of course, but also Catholics, Anglicans, liberals . . . enumerating the errors of others was a simpler business than anxiously scrutinizing the state of my own belief. I didn't know what I was talking about, of course—I was nineteen, and the joint rigors of my studies and my social life didn't give me much time to actually learn any real theology. But I did have a love/hate relationship with a little book called *Escape from Reason* by Francis Schaeffer, a dizzyingly brisk survey of Western philosophy, art, and culture from Thomas Aquinas to Timothy Leary, taking in Hegel, Barth, Cosimo de Medici, both Francis Bacons, Picasso, the Marquis de Sade, and a motley host of others.

The heart of Schaeffer's argument is that the writing was on the wall for Western culture as soon as Aquinas, following Aristotle, allowed a certain autonomy to human reason when it operates in the realm of nature. Once a line was drawn between an autonomous nature in the "lower storey" and grace in the "upper storey" nature gradually "swallowed up" grace, which became increasingly marginal and was eventually eliminated from the conceptual vocabulary of the West. But because man is incapable of living entirely in the purely deterministic lower storey, Schaeffer argues, he is compelled to repopulate the upper storey with alternatives to grace: concepts of freedom and meaning. To reach these requires a leap of irrational faith from the lower storey—where his reason tells him the unbearable truth that he is nothing more than a machine—across the "line of despair" to the upper storey, by means of art, poetry, modernist theology, drugs, eastern mysticism, or whatever comes to hand.

Schaeffer is no scholar: his knowledge of the history of philosophy is patently shallow, and he gets some things just plain wrong. But he is no fool either. He sketches the development of his key idea swiftly and smoothly, if not subtly, and neatly picks out and synthesizes its manifestations across a broad spectrum of contemporary cultural phenomena. As a pocket-sized polemical genealogy of '60s culture, the book has a certain flair. But he intends it not as a description but rather as a diagnosis of a fatal illness, to which he then produces a cure, in the form of the Bible, or the "biblical system," as he tellingly prefers to call it. For Schaeffer, any system of theology that treats the Bible as revealing divine truth poetically, metaphorically, or spiritually has sold out to the modern world and is hiding its despair behind a veneer of religious language with no actual content. The biblical system is composed of fully rational, interlocking propositions: direct representations in human language of absolute truth. Contrary to (Schaeffer's inaccurate view of) Aquinas, human intellect is completely fallen and must, like all of human life, be placed in absolute submission to this system. Only thus can the rot that entered the West with Aquinas be stopped. The biblical system, as propounded by Schaeffer, sweeps aside Dante and Hegel and Jaspers and Giacometti and Foucault: all of the strugglings and yearnings of Western philosophy and art are neatly dealt with and an unassailable, utterly rational system put in their place that will eliminate any further confusion.

When I first read Schaeffer I knew considerably less than he did about the thinkers and writers and artists whom he so abruptly dispatched. But I hoped someday to know more, and wanted there to be more to them than fundamental error leading to inevitable despair. The abruptness with which he handled them annoyed me even then. Schaeffer's lack of subtlety is, moreover, precisely the sort of thing that gives people an excuse to dismiss religious thought as outmoded, laughable, or contemptible. There has been a spate of books in recent years arguing that religious belief is inextricably entangled with dishonest, destructive patterns of thought and behavior and is a bane of which the modern world needs to rid itself. One of the most prominent books of the "new atheist" school is *The God Delusion* by Richard Dawkins. Dawkins, like Schaeffer, is no fool. Unlike Schaeffer, however, he *is* a scholar—an evolutionary biologist, and no doubt an excellent one. Certainly when he writes about science he is excellent; his explanations of evolutionary accounts of religion, of the anthropic principle, of meme theory, woven into the book are clear, elegant, often witty, and his treatment of the methods and marvels of scientific thought are measured and engaging.

But the purpose of the book is not to educate people about science but, as he avows openly in the preface, to turn religious readers into atheists—not agnostics, prepared to withhold judgment on the question of God's existence, but atheists. Dawkins begins with the assumption that the scientific form of knowledge is the only form. He quotes, only to dismiss, the position held by the majority of scientists that science *qua* science has simply nothing to say on the subject of religion, and insists that the "God Hypothesis" is thus a scientific theory susceptible to the same kinds and standards of evidence as theories about the physical world. Beginning from this position, as absurd to most religious thinkers as Schaeffer's claim that the Bible is the final source for knowledge of the physical world is to most scientists, he goes on to show that the God Hypothesis is a weak one, as there are scientific explanations for the existence of the universe, of life, of morality, of religion itself.

When Dawkins broaches anthropology, sociology, and moral philosophy, he is much the same as Schaeffer—a quick mind making swift, shallow, clever syntheses of ideas of which he has only passing knowledge. When he turns directly to religion, he becomes shrill, disorganized, and puerile. Although the God

Hypothesis seems merely to posit the existence of supernatural creative intelligence, in practice he concerns himself largely with the manifestation of that hypothesis among right-wing, young-earth creationist, fundamentalist American Protestants, with a sidelong glance at Islamic suicide bombers. His descriptions of religious belief and behavior are cobbled together, with no pretense of scholarly method or objectivity, largely on the basis of Internet searches, although he also introduces as evidence extracts from hate mail he has received from individuals who are clearly quite nuts, but whom he readily takes as typical representatives of religious believers. While Schaeffer feels pity for those he has placed below the line of despair, Dawkins feels an extraordinary contempt and dislike for those who embrace religious faith, who admit any form of knowing other than that which Dawkins himself excels at.

It might be rather fun to adjudicate an imaginary debate between Schaeffer and Dawkins but it would get absolutely nowhere. They speak entirely different conceptual languages and build their cases on the basis of radically incompatible axioms. Schaeffer would waste no time in describing Dawkins' error in Schaeffer's own terms. Dawkins would do the same to Schaeffer, and each would feel that the opponent had been decisively, indeed fatally, dispatched and that there was nothing more to say on the subject. I have brought them together not to settle the score between them, but merely to make the ironic point that Dawkins, in terms of intellectual temperament, is very much the same sort of beast as Schaeffer. Both stand in much the same relationship to ideas as Mme. Verdurin stands to her guests. Both have something to offer, just as Mme. Verdurin has a comfortable house with music and good food and occasionally interesting conversation. But all are possessed, and deformed, by a compulsive need for control. Mme. Verdurin cannot allow that her salon is one among many and that there is good food and music and conversation elsewhere in Paris that her guests might also enjoy. Neither Schaeffer nor Dawkins can tolerate the notion that rational, intelligent, decent people might be persuaded by arguments other than their own, or that there might be areas of life about which they simply do not know much, and should gracefully cede to others who are better informed than they. Not content to engage others with the things they are really good at, all of them resort to shrill, undignified, dishonest tactics in their hostile rejection of whatever they cannot bring under their control. Mme. Verdurin's absurd lie that the aristocratic patroness of a rival salon has to dole out cash to get anyone to attend her gatherings is scarcely more outrageous than some of the things that Schaeffer and Dawkins say about their intellectual opponents.

But when I was twenty this sort of world—of control, suspicion, and hostility—was the context for the intellectual part of my religious life, and as much as it chafed and irritated me, I didn't see any clearly marked alternatives. Then the summer before my final year my reading list included John Henry Newman's *Apologia pro vita sua*. I approached it with what I considered a wholesome suspicion in the spirit of Schaeffer. I knew that it was an account of his conversion to Catholicism, and was therefore of the enemy because Catholics patently weren't *real* Christians. I also knew that it was one of the classics of the language and I'm an absolute sucker for good prose: to this day if you can turn a good enough sentence you can persuade me, for the duration, that Elvis shot JFK and is now working at a Walmart in Missouri.

So, with my guard up, I set off into enemy territory and within twenty pages I had laid down arms and surrendered. I had by no means defected—the idea of going over to the other side hadn't entered my head, any more than it had entered Newman's at twenty pages. But I had left forever the hard smallness of the world that evangelicalism had been for me. I had tolerated it because I believed that the discomfort I felt was a necessary corollary of the sincerity, integrity, and commitment of real Christian faith. But it was impossible to doubt the sincerity, integrity, and commitment of Newman's faith, which was also broad, elegant, enticing, mysterious, compelling, thrilling and consoling by turns and all at once. There was no question of my writing him off, Schaeffer-like, as "not a Christian," and that meant there were possibilities in being a Christian that I hadn't dreamed of. I had no idea what to do about it, and there was nobody at home I could go to, so that summer I just rambled, wide-eyed, through the majestic elegance of Newman's sentences.

When I got back to Oxford I had to stop rambling and start thinking, both because I had essays to write, and because I had my own faith to deal with and orient to this new, expanded territory. Talking to the Catholics was still quite out of the question, but I found my way, one morning early in Michaelmas Term, to weekday mass in the little choir chapel at Pusey House, a chaplaincy at the High Church "smells and bells" end of the Church of England. For the rest of the year I went back three or four mornings a week, and stayed afterwards for tea and toast and marmalade with a cluster of students and four priests in long cassocks. I was enchanted. After the careless minimalism of CU meetings—carpet tiles, folding chairs, and guitar-choruses—the chilly gothic austerity and hushed chanting of weekdays and the incense and choir of Sunday high mass was strong wine; and even the quaint courteous tweed-and-sherry, Brideshead-inflected flavor of the Pusey crowd had a charm of its own that I rather liked.

I loved the place, but was still on my guard against being lured and seduced off the straight and narrow path by incense and chant, which plainly had nothing to do with truth. I went— anxious, plaintive, hopeful, and stubborn—to talk to the priests, and hit them with all the standard evangelical objections that I could muster to see what they could say. Father Philip would invariably wither me with a raised eyebrow and an acerbic snort and I would get all indignant because I knew exactly what he meant, and then I'd go see Father Stuart, who would affirm and reassure and sympathize and console. I don't know to what extent this good cop/bad cop act was a deliberate pastoral strategy on their part, but it worked like a treat for me and I adored them both.

The main thing I learned that year (apart from lots of fluffy trivia about cassocks and ombrellinos that I've long since forgotten) was that Christianity didn't exist primarily in my head. It existed in the world and in the church and in history, and if it was true it was true there, entirely regardless of whether or not I happened to believe it at any given moment. This came as revelation and liberation, which only goes to show how wrongheaded I had been before—I can remember acutely the delight and relief I felt when I asked Father Stuart whether he *knew* that he was saved, and he said, merrily, "Good heavens no! I know God's will will be done—how could I possibly know more than that?"

I also learned that it was perfectly alright to think of faith as a journey I was just beginning on, not something I had definitively attained to. I learned that there was no way I could figure it all out; much of Christianity was mystery and better expressed in liturgical rhythms of music and silence and speech and gesture and color than in tidy bullet points on a battered overhead projector. I also learned, incidentally and perhaps most importantly of all, that much of my unhappiness and anxiety as an evangelical had been self-imposed and largely nobody's fault but my own—when I mustered the courage to tell my CU friends that I had been consorting with the enemy, instead of the worry and disapproval I had been braced for I was met with friendly interest and acceptance, and a few people came along to Pusey with me and rather liked it.

After Oxford I crossed the Atlantic to grad school in the Religious Studies department of a state university. After the glowingly rich but unabashedly traditional world of the Oxford Eng. Lit. course, it was a sudden cold plunge into the Western intellectual tradition since the Enlightenment, and I was hit broadside by a world of brave new ideas: postmodernism and deconstruction and historicism and pluralism and the social construction of reality and the hermeneutical circle and what have you. Had I not stumbled onto Newman and into Pusey House the year before, either I would have retreated in horror or, more likely, my brittle narrow faith would have crumbled into shards around me, leaving me despairing, or bewildered, or angry, or contemptuous, or all four. As it was I joined an Episcopal parish with a sympathetic priest, and I went to church and went to class, and read my Bible and read Derrida and Nietzsche and Habermas and Schleiermacher and Kierkegaard and Tillich, and said my prayers and wrote my papers, and bobbed around in a great ocean of confusion, utterly lost most of the time but enjoying the ride.

Very loosely put, most of the ideas I encountered during those first years were clustered around the notion of contingency. This means, in brief, that our claims that we have observed, come to knowledge of, interpreted, and are now able to speak truth about reality are highly provisional because we have no stable ground where we can stand while doing our knowing and interpreting and speaking. We can see not from a neutral height but only from the perspective of a tiny corner in human history and culture; can understand not with pure universal reason but only with minds that are inescapably shaped by that corner, by our own experiences and temperaments, by assumptions so close to us that we don't even know they are there; can speak not in a universal, fundamental language, but only in the vocabulary and idiom available to us. Even the physical sciences are not entirely exempt from the contingency of knowledge, while claims to certain knowledge in the realms of philosophy, politics, ethics, and religion seem entirely helpless before the corrosive force of the central insight. The question, "But how do you *know* that?" is unanswerable; it leads either to a circular argument or to an endless regression of reasons and arguments: "Well, okay, but how do you know *that? And that?* . . ."

So we have, on one side, the controlling compulsion of those like Schaeffer and Dawkins who are determined that their own particular certainties and ways of knowing are the only ones. On the other side is surrender, by those who are aware primarily of their own inescapable smallness, who see absolutely no possibility of privileging their own ways of knowing over any other ways.

This surrender can be highly intelligent: rigorous, self-aware, nuanced—a calm acceptance that one's epistemological supply lines have been cut off and that one must make a measured retreat from "upper storey" positions that can no longer be sustained and regroup in the lower storey to consider one's options. On the other hand it can be a passive despair in the face of (rather than a clear-eyed understanding of) one's own limitations, an abnegation of responsibility for one's own ideas, a flight from the hard work of careful thought and from the challenge of constructive argument that expresses itself in the work of water-cooler platitudes: "It's all relative," "Everyone is entitled to their own opinion," "What's true for you may not be true for me," or fantasies about "creating your own reality" by force of imagination and will. As a society we are caught in the tug between control and surrender, between the desire for certainty and the awareness of contingency. We are enamored of opinions, our culture awash in pundits, blogs, op-ed columns, but at the same time we collectively extol "open-mindedness" as the supreme virtue and condemn "intolerance" as the worst of crimes. Thus anyone who makes any effort to cultivate some form of intellectual life (this *de facto* includes everybody reading this sentence) faces a predicament. We can inhabit a mountaintop fortress, barricaded by the authority of the Bible or the Koran, or by Marxist or libertarian ideology or some other self-contained system that offers the key to a certain understanding of everything. This sort of isolation is secure, but increasingly difficult to maintain. Should we admit the contingency of our knowledge, on the other hand, unbolt the door and step outside, we find ourselves on a precipitous and slippery slope that appears to lead down, on and on, with no clear footholds to arrest our descent into the void of utter relativity.

Is there an alternative to the isolation of control and the helplessness of surrender? What would it mean to practice hospitality in one's intellectual life, to offer genuine welcome to ideas, to open the mind to strange ideas, and yet to respect and nurture the mind's integrity? Can we hope to find an intellectual poise that will enable us to live with grace on the slope between the fortress and the void?

I think that we can, but that there is no formula. Minds, as my panicky courtship dream comically revealed, are in some ways like households. The physical furniture of a household all comes from somewhere and has a story. Our older daughters' beds, for instance, have held three families of cousins and cousins-in-law and were transported here from the Midwest in the van of a former student who had been canoeing with Glen between graduating with a degree in physics and entering the Franciscan novitiate. Our son's bed is the one my mom died in. The littlest's bed used to belong to the ex-boyfriend of my grad school roommate. And so on. Although I know such people exist, I don't personally know anyone so rich that they got to just go out and buy all their furniture to reflect their own tastes in perfect aesthetic harmony. Likewise I don't know anyone so clever that all their ideas are perfectly rational and coherent, but in this case I'm pretty sure there are no such people. Some of our ideas and convictions—what we think or believe or know—we carefully and deliberately acquired through reading, study, reflection. But even those of us who think for a living have a huge amount of mental furniture—of prejudices, loyalties, doubts, suspicions, anxieties, enthusiasms—that we pick up from infancy onwards, from family and friends, from the media, from the culture around us, without altogether realizing it, and that we fit together as best we can, getting so used to the result that we no longer notice that the chairs don't match or that the bathroom door sticks.

New ideas appear like guests at the doors of our minds. Some pass through and leave, but others hang around. Ideas have implications: like guests they bring baggage. Like guests they can be challenging and enriching, inconveniences and blessings all at once. Successful acts of welcome to ideas are as idiosyncratic as Joe and Linette's offbeat clutter, or the elderly puritans gathered around the French banquet, or the Garths' marriage. What makes these possible? In both cases there is something on which the integrity of the household hangs and that cannot be surrendered. What Mme. Verdurin will not compromise is her own needy ego, but for the Brotherhood and Mrs. Garth it is something larger than themselves; the sisters resign themselves to luxury because they had made a promise to Babette and could not break it, and Mrs. Garth accepts all the privations of life with her husband because she adores his virtue. I don't know what Joe and Linette's secret was, but there must have been some pivot to their extraordinary poise enabling them to be thoroughly themselves and yet so open to anybody who called to say, "Can I come for the weekend? Oh, and I'd like to bring three friends."

Because acts of hospitality to ideas are so individual, they are best expressed and understood in the form of stories, accounts of the ways in which individuals encountered and assimilated new ideas into the particularities of their own minds. The form of the story acknowledges the slippery slope of contingency; had we been born into other times or places, or to other parents, or had we gone to other schools and made other friends, we too would have been other. On the other hand the mere act of writing the story of one's intellectual development means that the author has not simply surrendered helplessly to every idea that has come his way, that he values both the integrity of his mind and the claims of the new ideas that have appeared at his door, that he has given careful consideration to those claims, has braved inconvenience and risk to do the right thing by them. Finally it implies that the author considers the particular ideas around which he has been prepared to rearrange his household to be worthy of reception elsewhere.

The story of intellectual development is a favorite postmodern genre—this book could, I suppose, be said to be an example. A much solider instance is Bart Ehrman's recent *God's Problem: How the Bible Fails to Answer Our Most Important Question—Why We Suffer*. Ehrman does two things. He outlines and illustrates biblical responses to the problem of evil, ways in which the text deals with the existence of suffering in a world created by a loving and all-powerful God. At the same time he tells the story of his own progression from devout evangelical (much of the sort that I was in college), to liberal theologian, to agnostic. The two strands of the book are closely bound together; he tries to reconcile the existence of God with the existence of evil but finds he cannot, and when he abandons the attempt he is forced to abandon also his faith. The pivot for Ehrman's intellectual and spiritual journey, the point on which he refuses to bend, is a deep horror at the realities of human suffering. He resists all attempts to tame this horror; when he came to the conclusion that all religious answers to the problem of evil are inadequate, that they do in fact tame or minimize or dodge the reality of evil and suffering, he finds himself forced to abandon his Christian faith.

As Ehrman tells it, the loss of his faith was and remains a source of deep sorrow to him. Although I disagree with his conclusions, I am inclined to sympathize with his story and to respect his integrity, in large part because he does not browbeat his reader, or try to construct an unassailable fortress around his own conclusions. Unlike Schaeffer and Dawkins, he admits readily that many conscientious, intelligent people do not reach the same conclusions. Concerning the problem of suffering, Ehrman writes that some of his friends, whom he describes as "brilliant,"

> realize why it's a religious problem for me but don't see it as a problem for themselves. In its most nuanced form . . . this view is that religious faith is not an intellectualizing system for explaining everything. Faith is a mystery and an experience of the divine in the world, not a solution to a set of problems.[1]

"I respect this view deeply," he continues, "and some days I wish I shared it." He holds no animus towards those who do, and insists, "I am not interested in destroying anyone's faith or deconverting people from their religion. I am not about to urge anyone

---

1. Ehrman, *God's Problem*, 15.

to become an agnostic."[2] Dawkins does not believe in God either, but he calls those who do "dyed-in-the-wool faith-heads," and declares that "if this book works as I intend, religious readers who open it will be atheists when they put it down."[3] Dawkins' book is a volley from a mountaintop fortress; Ehrman's, I think, is a good example of living with dignity and integrity and compassion on the slope.

I said that Ehrman's method—a blending of argument with personal narrative—is a distinctively postmodern genre, and indeed it is undergoing a particular vogue at present. But it is by no means an invention of our era; it has a distinguished ancestry. A few examples. C. S. Lewis, a scholar, convert, and apologist, was a conservative with a robust contempt for relativism, and in one of his best books he offers a scornful demolition of the kind of "honest doubt" that Ehrman proclaims.[4] Yet the 1958 memoir of his conversion to Christianity, *Surprised by Joy*, fully, indeed delightedly, acknowledges the myriad ways in which his thought was shaped by his temperament and his temperament by his early experiences. The "central story of my life," he says, the nonnegotiable, the pivot of his thought, is about what he calls Joy—an intense, bittersweet longing, "an unsatisfied desire which is itself more desirable than any other satisfaction."[5] The longing was first awakened in his childhood by trivial, homely, altogether contingent things—a line from Longfellow, a biscuit tin full of moss, *Squirrel Nutkin*—but he pursued it through voracious reading in classics and mythology, through an anxious, overscrupulous childhood Christianity, past a fascination with the occult, around atheism, through realism into idealism, losing sight of it, rediscovering it, attempting to grasp it only to find it slip though his fingers, and reappear elsewhere.

2. Ibid., 17.

3. Dawkins, *God Delusion*, 5.

4. See *Great Divorce*, chapter 5.

5. Lewis, *Surprised by Joy*, 17–18.

As Lewis matured and his thinking tightened and sharpened, he started to see, lurking behind the idea of the Absolute, the outlines of Spirit, and behind that the idea of a personal God. This was a deeply unwelcome idea; the Absolute was comforting to contemplate, but would make no demands, would never invade his cherished privacy, whereas God would arrive on his doorstep with baggage and demands and upset that privacy thoroughly, and he resisted conversion as vehemently as Martine and Philippa had resisted sensual indulgence. But as the sisters were compelled by the habit of duty to accept the alarming intrusion of Babette's feast, so was Lewis compelled by the habit of deductive reasoning to accept the equally alarming intrusion of belief. The claims first of theism and eventually of Christianity pressed on him with increasing force; he admitted their claims, opened the door and resigned himself to a thorough overturning of his domestic arrangements: "I gave in, and admitted that God as God, and knelt and prayed: perhaps, that night, the most dejected and reluctant convert in all England."[6] The results were as fruitful as the transformation of the Brotherhood's life; Lewis welcomed God into a mind with a deep and rich character and integrity of its own, richly furnished by myth and literature and love of nature, of home comforts and of friendship: a mind that created Narnia and other worlds besides.

Further back along the trail is Newman's *Apologia*, the book that blew the doors open for my restless (and largely uncomprehending) twenty-year-old self. Newman was at the center of a hugely influential movement to resist the encroachments of liberal thought in England by asserting that the Church of England represented the true inheritance of the early church, and when his reading and study in the Fathers of the church drew him to Rome, it was a devastating blow to the Church of England. It was an even more devastating blow to Newman himself, but it was one he could not dodge. He freely admits the myriad contingencies of his story; some of its most dramatic turning points hang

6. Ibid., 228–29.

on the slenderest occurrences—a passing comment by an acquaintance, a sentence that catches his attention. But this fragile web of books he might not have read, people he might not have met, conversations he might not have had, gradually solidified into a conviction that Rome was, after all, the true Church and that despite the agonizing rupture of loyalties, his place lay there.

All stories of this sort, that bear witness to the disruption, transformation, pain, and enrichment that ideas can bring when they appear on our doorsteps, are highly individual, bearing the distinctive marks of their own periods and of the individual mental spaces whose histories they reflect. All of them, however, carry through the centuries the DNA of the mother of all intellectual autobiographies, the *Confessions* of St. Augustine, who was born in North Africa during the last years of the Roman Empire. Augustine's twenties were spent among the Manichees, a sect that propagated an elaborate mythology about the material world in entire disregard of contemporary science, and who taught that God was a material substance, in perpetual war with an evil counterpart. Then he was for a time a skeptic, disbelieving (not unlike Dawkins) in the possibility of any knowledge other than the purely scientific, and after that he experimented with neo-Platonic mysticism, which he also found unsatisfactory. Through all of this he was drawn on (not unlike Ehrman, but with different results) by the problem of evil. At the same time he was dealing with the rest of life: with love and sex and marriage, with career and money and ambition, with friendship and recreation and temptation and grief, and with his mother, to whose floods of tearful prayers he attributes his salvation, but who must have been extraordinarily irritating at times. As Augustine tells his story he digresses continually, weaving into every episode reflections on its meaning from the perspective of the Christian faith to which it brought him. His own, contingent experiences, the quirks of his own personality, blossom into mini-treatises; his passion for the theater into a reflection on the pleasure found in the artistic representation of suffering; a chance encounter with a drunk beggar into a discourse on the perversity of ambition; and an episode in which he and a gang of friends steal some pears from a neighbor's garden, famously, into a consideration of human motivation and in particular of the reasons why we so consistently make bad self-defeating decisions when we know better.

Augustine's intellectual quest eventually brought him to accept the validity of Christian teaching, but the implications of that teaching for the rest of his life kept him from conversion—he believed that Christianity was true but, like Lewis, he knew that to welcome the teaching that Christ is Lord would involve a massive reorganization of his life and demand that he let go of lots of things he didn't want to let go of. Finding the truth was no longer his problem; his own will was his problem, and he was miserable until, one summer day in a garden, a child's voice chanting "take up and read" lead him to a passage from Romans; he read it, and "it was as if a light of relief from all anxiety flooded into my heart."[7] The inner struggle between intellect and will was over. Augustine went on to become Bishop of Hippo, and to write a flood of texts that form the foundations of the great edifice of medieval theology, and are inescapably influential to this day.

The DNA of the *Confessions* manifests itself in myriad ways in Christian theology, psychology, and literature. Aquinas depends on him, as do Luther, Freud, and Dostoyevsky. Newman and Ehrman are his descendants. Augustine himself understands and accepts that intellectual influence is a complicated business. Ideally, he says we should read trustworthy authors, encounter in them true ideas, recognize them as such, and welcome them as our own. But Augustine knows that it rarely works this way, that the business of communicating and transferring ideas is a precarious one, perpetually prone to misfiring, that we are very likely to misread and misunderstand authors, their intentions and their ideas, and that even when we do learn something true from an author who speaks the truth, we are likely to give it a different

7. Augustine, *Confessions*, 8.12.29 (Chadwick, 153).

function and position in our mental world than it did in his. But as messy and full of slippage (and of the near-inevitability of error) as the process of intellectual influence is, it is fertile. In fact "the whole benefit of reading," Augustine says, lies in the sort of fruitful mistake we make when we "understand some truth from another's writing, which the writer himself did not understand."[8] The most "honorable" method of reading, he says, is to assume the best that we can of an author's character and intentions, and to feel free to rearrange in our own minds what we glean from them in our own search for truth.

From Augustine, one of the greatest minds in the two-thousand-year history of Christianity, back, absurdly, to me, probably not one of the greatest minds in the last hour and a half. However, as I started with my own story, I should, briefly, wrap it up. When I met Glen early in grad school I was an Anglican of recent pedigree, and he was an increasingly discontented Lutheran. It was clear to both of us that if we were to be married we'd have to be in the same church, and it was clear to both of us that the Catholic Church is the default setting for Christians in the West and that that was where we should be. I was, as luck, grace, and the vagaries of the academic market would have it, hired by a Jesuit university; as soon as we moved here, we joined the Rite of Christian Initiation for Adults (RCIA) program at the local cathedral and were received on the following Easter.

The process was less reluctant and wrenching than Ehrman's or Lewis's, Newman's or Augustine's, but it wasn't tidy and it certainly wasn't triumphant. To be perfectly honest, I'm not wild about all of contemporary American Catholicism. I don't like the halfhearted music and the slovenly preaching, and some of the theological idiom grates, and until the day I die I will probably be nostalgic for Pusey House, for dust motes in sunbeams through

---

8. Augustine, *Usefulness of Belief,* 4.10 (Burleigh, 298). *The Usefulness of Belief* is an anti-Manichee treatise addressed to an old friend whom he had led into the sect and now hopes to lead out again. Augustine never forgot the experiences and errors and loyalties of his younger self, which continued to shape his mature thought.

gothic windows, for the somber dignity of Anglican chant, even, idiotically, for the sherry and tweed. But being Catholic rather than Protestant means precisely that one does not base one's religious allegiance on personal judgment, let alone on aesthetic and cultural taste. I'll doubtless always grumble a bit, but I'm not going anywhere.

It's not unlike how I feel about our house. I complain constantly about the clutter, but it's home and I have no intention of moving. Oddly, perhaps, my messy housekeeping reflects my intellectual more than it does my neater emotional life. Actually, this is a shameful state of affairs for someone who is supposedly a Christian intellectual: I should err on the side of tolerance and generosity in my dealings with people and, in my dealings with ideas, on the side of rigor. But instead I am inclined to be bossy and controlling in personal relationships, like Mme. Verdurin and Rosamund, walled up in the tidy fortress of my own willfulness, whereas intellectually I am naturally more like Moshe and Malli, standing by helplessly while new ideas force entry and never really calling them to account. I'm no more satisfied with this than I am with the tangle of socks, lightsabers, and dust bunnies that seems to have taken up squatters' rights at the top of the stairs, but it is what it is; this is the only home I have, and if I am to welcome people and ideas, this is where I have to do it.

Hospitality, real welcome to ideas as well as to people, demands both openness to the stranger at the gates and respect for the integrity of one's interior space, for its principles of consistency and order. Ehrman, Lewis, and Newman are all prepared to make room in their minds to ideas that cause them distress and demand sacrifice, but there are lines they will not cross, ideas that they will not countenance. Ehrman rejects whatever appears to minimize the monstrosity of human suffering, Lewis accepts only ideas that are both logically rigorous and make room for the experience of Joy, Newman rejects utterly the "principle of private judgement." And Augustine, the ancestor of us all, offers a principle that is broader and simpler, but more devastatingly demanding than all of these: the great commandment of love. Learning, reading, interpreting is a messy business, but the best understanding of a text or idea is that which is most conducive to love and knowledge of God and neighbor.[9] In Augustine's time the end of the Roman Empire appeared as an earthquake that threatened to destroy the fabric of human society; in ours a tsunami of contingency threatening to sweep away not only all particular certainties but the very possibility of certainty itself. For both times, perhaps for all times, love of God and neighbor can teach us, as it taught Martine and Philippa and the Garths, to live with grace and poise on the slippery slope.

In considering the notion of welcome to ideas, I have dealt primarily with religious ideas, as they are the ones I understand best. Religion *does* involve ideas and the usual baggage they bring, and the intellectual aspect of conversion is certainly interesting. But religious ideas are different from political or scientific ideas because they all point beyond themselves; Christianity specifically says that behind all doctrines is a person, standing at the door and knocking, and that conversion is not just about welcoming ideas but about welcoming a relationship. Lewis and Newman and Augustine are explicit about this. All describe themselves as being moved by a power entirely outside of themselves. Lewis, describing the last months of his resistance, calls God "my Adversary" and his conversion, his "checkmate."[10] Newman prays for God's "kindly light" to lead him on amid the "encircling gloom" of doubt and confusion. Augustine frames his entire book as a letter to God, who pursued and won him. All have no doubt that behind their transactions with ideas lies a will other than their own.

In the final chapter we will look at what it means to welcome, and to be welcomed by, God, and at how hospitality functions as a metaphor in biblical and spiritual writing. In the meantime, we

9. Augustine, *On Christian Doctrine*, 1.36.40 and 3.10.15.
10. Lewis, *Surprised by Joy*, 216.

will return to the less metaphorical sort of hospitality—the sort that involves bringing people into a physical space.

4

I Was a Stranger

Hospitality and the World

I have used Francis Schaeffer's *Escape from Reason* as a negative example, as an instance of control, as a failure of true hospitality to ideas. But although I don't think much of his approach to ideas, I owe Schaeffer and his wife Edith a great debt of gratitude. Together they founded and ran the community of L'Abri, in Switzerland, which was where Joe and Linette met.

As Edith Schaeffer tells the story, L'Abri just sort of happened.[1] The family went to Switzerland as missionary pastors, a few people came to visit, came back bringing friends, word spread, more people came, they outgrew their original chalet, bought more property in the neighborhood, became an informal stop on the intellectual hippy trail of the '60s, instituted a training program, and twenty-five years after Schaeffer's death there are L'Abri communities on five continents where "it is still possible to share in the life of an 'extended family' as was the case when L'Abri first began."[2] Joe and Linette's house was not formally one of these but, in deciding to open their home to the likes of my friends and me, they must have

1. See Edith Schaeffer, *L'Abri*.
2. L'Abri Fellowship International, "L'Abri Today."

taken their cue, to some extent, from L'Abri. So, as far as I now am from Schaeffer's theological influence, I remain a sort of distant descendant. I expect there are lots of us.

Although the Schaeffers felt they were making it up as they went along, they were by no means the first Christians to make a priority of welcoming strangers. Hospitality was of enormous importance in the first Christian centuries. In the pagan world into which the Church was born, hospitality had been a means of strengthening the bonds and reaffirming the patterns of a stratified society; people played host to those whom they thought could help them. The way the first Christians thought about and practiced hospitality flew in the face of this tradition. Christians saw themselves as accountable to the example of Abraham and, of course, to the words of Jesus. In Matthew's parable of the sheep and goats, Jesus describes the Son of Man welcoming into the kingdom those who he says had fed him when he was hungry, visited him when he was sick, or taken him in when he was a stranger, and sends away those who rejected him. Both groups are puzzled. "When did we see you hungry? When did we meet you as a stranger?" they ask, and he shows them the meaning, the pattern of all the choices of their lives: "Truly I tell you, just as you did it to one of the least of those who are members of my family, you did it to me."

The idea that God is in every needy person we encounter presented a radical challenge: it ran right against the grain of habit and culture, and the early Church struggled with it. James had harsh words for Christians who had already allowed the social distinctions and values of the world around them to creep into their community and worship, treating the wealthy with honor and the poor with disdain, offering the best seats to the well dressed and telling the ragged to sit on the floor. This sort of behavior, he tells them, calls into question their very faith. "Do you with your acts of favoritism really believe in our glorious Lord Jesus Christ?" he asks, and reminds them that it is with the poor that Jesus identifies.

It was a challenge, indeed, but one that Christians could not avoid: there was no getting round Jesus' words "I was a stranger, and you took me in . . . for as you did it to one of the least of those who are members of my family, you did it to me." In sermon after sermon, the early Church Fathers—Clement of Alexandria, Ambrose, Gregory of Nyssa, John Chrysostom, Jerome—cite these words and exhort their readers and hearers to remember that hospitality is a sacred duty.[3] The church conceived the practice of hospitality as an act of obedience to the words of their Lord rather than an as experiment in social engineering, but the call to recognize Christ in the needy stranger, to despise distinctions of wealth and status, and to build their community and social relations with a view to the coming of the Kingdom rather than to the shoring up of the status quo, had immense effects on the society around them.[4] The pagan Emperor Julian recognized that Christian practices, although motivated by a faith that he despised and hoped to eliminate, were superior to the old traditions and presented a serious obstacle to his goal of restoring the worship of the old gods. "It is disgraceful" he lamented, that because "the impious Galileans support not only their own poor but ours as well, all men see that our people lack aid from us,"[5] and he instructed that priests set up pagan institutions to care for strangers and the needy. Faith in Christ had led to such unarguably significant and admirable social changes that Julian hoped that by emulating his enemies' religion his own might be revitalized.

Julian's project failed, and with it the old order: the Roman Empire crumbled under its own weight and the pressure of invading tribes. In its wake the church faced the glorious opportunity of building a new society founded on the Gospel and faced,

3. See Oden, *And You Welcomed Me.*

4. In this account of the history of Christian hospitality, and in much of the first half of this chapter, I am very heavily indebted to Christine Pohl's *Making Room: Recovering Hospitality as a Christian Tradition.* I make a hesitant attempt in this chapter to synthesize into a very short space some of her main arguments, and I heartily recommend the book as a whole.

5. Quoted in Pohl, *Making Room,* 43–44.

with it, the withering temptations to compromise and corruption that come with power and property, with being at the center instead of on the margins. Crucial to the church's task, especially in the early centuries after the fall of Rome, were the monasteries, and crucial to the monasteries was the mission of hospitality. The Rule that Benedict of Nursia drew up to govern the monastery at Monte Cassino in around 540, and that sets the basic pattern of religious life to this day, is clear on this, referring explicitly to the examples of strangers, the poor, and the sick. Every monastery should have a guest house with sufficient beds that whoever arrives can be received like Christ, "for he is going to say 'I came as a guest and you received me.'"[6] The monastery should by no means permit the sort of "respect of persons" according to worldly status that James condemns; rather special care should be given to the poor, with whom Christ particularly identifies himself, and special space and food devoted to the care of the sick.

The structures that descend from these monastic practices are with us to this day, but the distance between Benedict's world and our own can be seen in the fact that it probably does not occur to us to notice that "hospital," "hospice," and "hospitality" are essentially the same word. The first two we associate with the public world of institutions, the last with the private domestic world, and we experience the gap between these as huge. The gap has been in existence, and has been widening, for a long time; according to Pohl, by the time of the Reformation, "two trajectories of hospitality—hospitality as material care for strangers and the local poor and hospitality as personal welcome and entertainment—had developed along largely separate tracks"[7] pulling the meaning of everyday words apart as they went. "Charity," among Christians, used to mean love for God and neighbor. Now, even among Christians, it usually means writing a check to the United Way. A secular language of human rights, of social justice and solidarity has gradually grown

6. Pohl, *Making Room*, 53
7. Ibid., 51.

out of the language of the gospel and pursued a parallel track, and many social institutions, values, and policies that have their roots in Matthew, James, and Benedict are now in the hands of people who are indifferent or even hostile to Christianity but who, like Julian, recognize and embrace as fundamental goods some of the same things that Christians embrace.

There are very significant goods in this state of affairs. Philosophical issues aside (I have no intention of getting entangled in the question of whether Western society can sustain itself in the long run once detached from its religious roots), it is simply the case that some kinds of care can be provided more effectively on a larger scale, supported by formal structures, informed by specialized skills and professional expertise. And that a society that acknowledges its responsibility for its needy members and builds institutions around that responsibility is an excellent thing, regardless of its religious culture and of the language in which it speaks about that responsibility. The "sheep" of Matthew 25 were as surprised when they learned whom they had welcomed as were the goats when they learned whom they had neglected: what mattered to the Son of Man was that the least of his brethren, those with whom he identified himself, had been welcomed and fed and cared for.

There are significant goods in the current situation, then, but there are also significant problems. First, of course, societal solidarity with the needy is by no means universal, nor is provision complete, by a long shot. The poor are, emphatically, still with us, even in the prosperous cities of the West. And even to the extent that our social institutions become just and effective, even to the extent that they meet the needs of the poor and the sick, there are needs that, by their very nature, they will always fail to meet. By Pohl's account this failure has itself a long history. By the end of the Middle Ages, she says, "in the diversity of institutions, in the loss of the worshiping community as a significant site for hospitality, and in the differentiation of care among recipients, the socially transformative potential of hospitality was lost."[8]

The gap between the two "trajectories of hospitality" and the resulting loss of hospitality's power to transform society is particularly acute in the case of the stranger. A stranger is one who is strange, estranged, alienated, someone who does not have a secure place in a world of relationships: of family, friendship, work, community, citizenship. An acute example is that of the homeless man on the city bench; the person who has no place, no person, no group where he belongs. What is my relationship and responsibility to him? I find myself overwhelmed and frightened by his need, but ironically also reassured by it—what, after all, can I do? I throw him a tight-lipped smile as I hurry by on the way to the next bit of my busy life telling myself (with little conviction) that I pay my taxes, I bear his needs rather than my own convenience in mind when I vote, I donate to the United Way and to the Salvation Army, and I tell myself that I have met my responsibility to him by putting it into the hands of people much better qualified than myself to help.

It is true that there are services available to him, agencies that can provide shelter, food, help for illness or addiction. But even if those services were adequate—and they almost certainly aren't—they could do nothing about his strangeness, because the particular needs of the stranger are acutely personal, and agencies are, by their nature, impersonal. Social service agencies have, since the '30s, been increasingly characterized by professionalization and bureaucratization. They have policies, intake forms, standardized methods developed by professionals for processing clients and assigning categories according to what sort of issues and problems they present, so that those issues and problems can be dealt with effectively. These policies and procedures are what enable them to do their job, but they also make it impossible for them to heal strangeness.

---

8. Ibid., 51.

The social worker who is trying to find a homeless person a place in a shelter, as well the person who drew up the intake form she is using, may herself be a deeply compassionate person. She probably is: it is likely that she could be making more money doing something less demanding and less useful and that she has chosen this career out of genuine human concern, perhaps as a direct response to Matthew 25. Nevertheless it is a career, with a salary and limited working hours, and regardless of her personal motivation the fact that she is being paid to have the conversation and will go home when her shift is over cannot fail to be a determining factor in the relationship, just as Mme. Verdurin's neediness is the determining factor in all of hers. If the only person who sits down with you and asks you questions about yourself is paid to do so, then you are really a stranger.

If agencies cannot heal the strangeness of the stranger, then what can? Nothing but a place where he knows people will be genuinely glad to see him. If I really care about the man on the bench, I need to let him know that he can invite himself over for dinner and a movie, crash on the couch, and raid the refrigerator for breakfast in the morning. There are plenty of people who know they are welcome in this way (I've lost track of the number of people who've had copies of our front door key), but he's definitely not one of them. Who knows where that would lead? It could well be dangerous. It is simply beyond my capacities to offer him the kind of personal welcome he needs; the best I could do would be to treat him as a pawn in a transaction between myself and God, as Moshe did with his guests. And if I make a heroic surrender of this sort, I will quickly be overrun, out of my depth. I have young children and our household has limits and rules, and if they are broached we'll end up in the kind of mess that Moshe and Malli did.

But this is no good. The sheep in Matthew 25, the early Christians who shamed the society around them by their welcome of all, had families and homes and limits too, and it didn't let it stop them. Clearly I have bought into pervasive American, consumerist, individualist assumptions that have warped my vision: I no longer see Jesus even in the precise places that he has told me he is to be found. And so on. And on and on and on, *ad nauseam*, getting neither me nor the guy on the bench anywhere.

The problem here is, in part, one of scale: the gulf between the complexity of modern society and the vastness of human need, on the one hand, and on the other, the resources of an individual, is too big for us—for me, at any rate—to wrap our heads around, and tends to send us spinning into this sort of unproductive flailing. To get some real traction on the relationship between material needs and the need for recognition and belonging, we need an intermediary position, a stepping stone, and a place between the institution and the individual, between control and surrender, where we can find balance, the poise that is at the heart of real welcome. This place of balance can be provided by communities that are big enough to have some stability and consistency to their practices but small enough that they can offer real belonging. The sisters could take the destitute refugee Babette into their home, and allow her to have a home in her world and still remain herself, because they had been raised and formed in community, in mutual responsibility and care.

There have always been Christian communities, committed to living together and finding in the patterns of common life the stability to resist the force of the surrounding culture that would sweep away the individual. The Rule of Benedict provided the template for a host of religious orders—Franciscans, Carmelites, Dominicans, Jesuits—bound together by the desire to live a common mission and vision. The Beguines, the Bruderhof, the Amish created new patterns of community life. In the last century a number of new communities have been formed, many of them with the specific mission of recovering the practice of hospitality, and it is perhaps in them that a way can be found to reunite the two trajectories of hospitality.

One of the most notable and influential of these new forms of community is the Catholic Worker Movement. The Catholic

Worker was born in Depression-era New York, where the itinerant activist Peter Maturin tracked down communist-turned-Catholic journalist Dorothy Day and informed her that she would help him propagate his ideas and carry out his reforming program. Part of this program was his determination to revive a Christian ministry of personal hospitality against the background of the institutional shelter provided by the Municipal Lodging House, what Day called "the largest bedroom in the world," with its seventeen hundred beds: "the collectivization of misery."[9] As Peter Maurin put it in his idiosyncratic style (not only did he write in the form of "Easy Essays," he spoke in the same form, all the time, to whoever happened to be in the room):

> people no longer
> > consider hospitality to the poor
> > as a personal duty
>
> And it does not disturb them a bit
> > to send them to the city
> > where they are given the hospitality
> > of the "Muni"
> > at the expense of the taxpayer
>
> But the hospitality that the "Muni"
> > gives to the down and out
> > is no hospitality
> > Because what comes from the taxpayer's
> pocketbook
> > does not come from his heart.[10]
>
> The Catholic unemployed
> > should not be sent to the Muni
>
> The Catholic unemployed
> > should be given hospitality
> > in Catholic Houses of Hospitality . . .

9. Day, *House of Hospitality*, 19.

10. Ibid., xxi–xxii.

We need Houses of Hospitality
> to give the rich
> the opportunity to serve the poor

We need Houses of Hospitality
> to show what idealism looks like
> when it is practiced.

The "idealism" in question, which remains at the heart of the Catholic Worker today, was Peter Maurin's philosophy of personalism, a philosophy

> which regards the freedom and dignity of each person as the basis, focus and goal of all metaphysics and morals. In following such wisdom we move away from a self-centered individualism toward the good of the other. This is to be done by taking personal responsibility for changing conditions, rather than looking to the state or other institutions to provide impersonal "charity." We pray for a Church renewed by this philosophy and for a time when all those who feel excluded from participation are welcomed with love, drawn by the gentle personalism Peter Maurin taught.[11]

The person is the center of all meaning and value, and is always to be welcomed and treated as such, never as a problem to be categorized, solved, and dealt with. Following Maurin's vision, this idealism takes the form of Houses of Hospitality, places where volunteer Workers live together with the destitute, the homeless, the stranger, sharing their poverty, their food, their space, their noise, their dirt. The strangeness of the stranger—the intractable strangeness that the most efficient institutions cannot heal and can only exacerbate—is met by such a house. Voluntary poverty, "casting our lot freely with those whose impoverishment is not a choice,"[12] heals the alienation that poverty brings with it

11. "Aims and Means of the Catholic Worker."
12. Ibid.

by creating new spaces in which poverty is the norm rather than an estrangement from it.

At the same time as healing strangeness, the Houses of Hospitality seek to revive the "socially transformative potential" of hospitality that Pohl said was eroded by the late Middle Ages. They not only reject the model of rehabilitation, whose goal is to diagnose and fix the needs of "clients" so that they can become like the rest of us and fit into the world around them, they also reject the values and patterns of that world, a society shaped by competition, violence, fear, warped by specialization and marked throughout by alienation. By working with the idea of hospitality rather than that of rehabilitation, Worker houses try to challenge that society by creating in miniature a different kind of society, one in which it is "easier to be good," built around welcoming people as they are.

Dorothy Day's accounts of the early years in the New York house are a vivid picture of a world from which strangeness has been banished by the simple act of making it the norm. Innumerable stories weave through the pages. They are not sermon-illustrations with satisfying, uplifting conclusions; the lives of the poor are full of bitter hardships, and their stories are of suffering—material hardship, frustration, injustice, squalor, anger, chaos, exhaustion, physical and mental illness. But they are stories of people, of individuals brought together into a common "we." It is often impossible to tell from Day's stories who is on what "side," or indeed that there is any gap between the "normal" people who run the place and the strangers they are looking after. The only norm is hardship and everybody shares it equally. Neither Dorothy Day nor Peter Maurin, who in a normal organization would have titles and offices and secretaries and dental benefits, even has their own room. Everybody is part of the "we"—there is a profound sense of a community in which strangeness has been dissolved by being embraced and shared.

Poverty is estranging in a society that places great value on wealth: in a thousand ways the poor are denied full participation in the world around them. But many other things can make a person a stranger also. As well as material wealth, our society values achievement, success, accomplishment, and talent, and people who lack the resources to care for themselves, let alone to compete, find not only their value as citizens but also their very worth as human beings called into question. Until fairly recently the kind of hospitality provided to people with mental disabilities was downright barbaric: they were often warehoused their entire lives in grim institutions, locked away from any form of participation in society, denied any possibility of developing personalities and talents. In 1964 Jean Vanier, a former naval officer, bought a primitive house in a French village and invited two men from a nearby institution for people with mental disabilities to come and share it with him. "Without any big vision (that's not my way)," he recounts, "it seemed quite clear that Jesus wanted me to do something." From these radically humble beginnings has grown L'Arche, an international network of "family-like homes" in which

> people with and without disabilities share their lives together, give witness to the reality that persons with disabilities possess inherent qualities of welcome, wonderment, spirituality, and friendship.[13]

Like the Catholic Worker, whose aim is to create a society in which it is easier to be good, the vision of L'Arche is not confined to providing care for people with disabilities but encompasses a broader vision of human life.

> Perhaps an extraordinary notion in our fast-paced and consumer-driven society, L'Arche believes that these qualities, expressed through vulnerability and simplicity, actually make those with a disability our real teachers about what is most important in life: to love and to be loved.[14]

13. L'Arche USA, "L'Arche USA."
14. Ibid.

I have myself been welcomed by L'Arche. Journey, one of a network of L'Arche houses in Erie, Pennsylvania, let me come for an overnight visit. When I arrived, it was mid-afternoon, and nobody was there except the live-in assistant; three of the core members were at their jobs, and the fourth was expected back any minute from a weekend hospitalization. Alice arrived first, still drugged-up, muzzy, and confused: she grinned broadly and silently when introduced to me, and went promptly off to sleep in her chair. She woke up long enough to make it to the kitchen when the van, driven by a seraphic college kid with big blue studs in his ears, arrived bringing the others home from work. They descended on her with great excitement and then noticed me. Dustin shook hands and introduced himself with precise and formal courtesy, Mike hugged me and said something that sounded for all the world Chinese. Jenny ignored me and started complaining about something I couldn't understand at all, until she vanished to the room she shared with Alice, came back with a pair of slippers, plopped herself on the floor at her friend's feet to take off her shoes and put on the slippers, protesting noisily all the while, it seemed to me, that Alice hadn't been properly taken care of.

When Alice was settled I asked about the piano in the hall. Dustin invited me to come listen and played something from *The Sound of Music,* which he had figured out himself, perfectly, as apparently he can do with anything he hears. It's a gift I envy greatly and one that complements my own, less impressive random talent of remembering all the lyrics to absolutely everything; we were working our way happily through all the songs, with Dustin playing a great deal better than I ever hope to sing and both of us having a grand time until Martin, the lad with the blue ears, suggested that as it was Dustin's day to make dinner perhaps we could wrap it up.

The two of them got to work breading the chicken fingers, while Mike set the table, chatting cheerfully to me in an idiom that started to sound a bit less like Chinese and a bit more like something I could learn to understand with practice. Dustin brought the food to the table, Martin dished up and we all ate, except for Alice who couldn't stay awake. Mike cleared and wiped the table, vacuumed around the table, and took out the trash. Jenny was on dishwashing duty but, after the fuss she had made of Alice, she got in a sad and jealous mood about the fuss the others were now making of her, refused to eat her dinner, and stomped off to her room. The rest of us said prayers around the table, then Martin and Tom (a big, gruff, ironic chap who had appeared while Dustin and I were in mid-*Edelweiss*) went after Jenny and gently insisted, remonstrated, bargained, and cajoled her out. She finally got it together and did the dishes in high spirits, with frequent breaks to chase Martin around with handfuls of lather. The whole thing took over an hour. Then Dustin came back to do the pots and pans while Mike was getting ready for his shower: a process that, for reasons I never grasped, was understood by all to take about another hour. Eventually the debate that had been going on intermittently and amicably all evening about what show they would watch was settled and we watched an episode of *All in the Family*.

Apart from that half an hour with Archie Bunker pretty much the whole six hours between the initial flurry of arrival and bedtime was taken up in one way or another with getting dinner on the table and cleaning up afterwards. If Martin and Tom had stuck everyone in front of the TV and done it themselves it would have taken about forty-five minutes—infinitely more efficient. But efficiency wasn't the point. The point was that it was Dustin and Jenny and Mike's home and therefore the chores were their chores. Everybody had a job to do and, once Jenny got past her meltdown, they did them—really, *really* slowly, but smoothly, carefully, tranquilly and with beautiful results: the house was pristine and pretty and peaceful. Nothing about the place—a big bungalow in a tidy suburb—suggested an institution: the only indications that it was anything other than a conventional family home were the fat binders full of forms tucked away in a corner

(L'Arche houses have to work hard to make sure that their obligations to be state-licensed facilities don't get in the way of their
vocations to be homes) and the great big fence that the people
next door had slapped up when their campaign to keep L'Arche
out of the neighborhood had failed.

It was a lovely place and a thoroughly pleasant evening. The
only false note was me. I was shy and awkward, which is not my
normal style at all. Now I'm not like the next door neighbors;
I don't find people with disabilities frightening. I can see why
one might, but I don't and I was perfectly happy being there as
a guest and eating dinner and hanging out and chatting. What
made me edgy was that I was there not just to hang out but to
ask questions and learn things and come home and write this
chapter. I asked Mike and the others some questions over dinner
but couldn't make much headway understanding the answers. I
looked to Martin and Tom for help, hoping for a "What Jenny
is saying is . . ." but they were placidly eating their dinner and
keeping an eye on Alice, who kept dropping off. I didn't like to
ask *them* questions, although they kept telling me I could. The
reason for my hesitancy was my sense that as carefully and ten-
derly and wisely as the community at Journey was constructed
and nurtured, it must, surely, be fragile. Surely, I thought, if I
were to start talking to Martin and Tom, the distinction between
the L'Arche people and the outsider passing through for a night,
would instantly be overlayed by the much starker, deeper, more
real gulf between an "us" who were "normal" and could stand on
our own feet—graduate college, drive cars, balance checkbooks,
navigate through life and careers, compete in the world—and a
"them" who weren't, and couldn't, and were dependent on the
intelligence and forbearance of "us." And surely it would be rude
for "us" to talk about "them" in front of them, but there was no
office or staff lounge where we could talk frankly in private: just a
kitchen and a dining room and a living room like there would be
in any suburban family house.

So that was my problem, but after about the fourth time that Tom said, "Don't you have any questions?" I decided I had to get over myself. "So, tell me about your story with L'Arche," I began lamely (one thing I learned from the experience was that I'd make a really bad journalist). "How did you start to work here? What do you like about it?" He told me that he had come to work there when he was in college simply because he needed a paycheck and it was the job he got. Since then he had got a degree and a professional job. "But by then these guys were my friends and I couldn't just leave, so I work here a couple of evenings a week just to see everybody. My other job pays a lot more, but I've got relationships here now, you know?" Now I could, just barely, see myself getting used to the glacial pace of the chores and learning to relax and grow past my anxiety for efficiency and control. I could certainly see myself getting fond of Dustin and Mike and Jenny and Alice, all of whom had been kind and welcoming in their different ways. But no way could I see myself ever thinking of them as the kinds of friends I would drive forty-five minutes to spend the evening with after a tiring day at work. "How do you get there?" I asked. "I mean, everybody here's really nice, but I don't get it. How do you get to where they are real friends, people you have relationships with rather than people you have responsibilities to?"

He chuckled. "Ah, the agency approach. Yeah, we all struggle with that at the start—to be honest, I still do, sometimes—but in L'Arche it's the enemy. Agencies talk about 'clients' and 'staff' and those are dirty words around here. Hard to say how one gets beyond it, really. Everyone's development goes at a different pace and some assistants just never get it and don't last long." Tom, rather to his own surprise, had "got it" and now thought of Journey as a community to which he really belonged, not as a community at which he worked. In one sense it was true that he and I belonged to an "us" of "normal" people, but inside the house it was irrelevant. The "us" of Journey transcended that division, and I was the stranger they were all welcoming together. As soon as I realized that, I was much more comfortable.

To help them on the path to a deeper belonging, all assistants at L'Arche have three levels of what is called accompaniment. The first, functional accompaniment, is what in an agency would be called training: what goes where, who needs what sort of help, how records are kept, how medication is handled, that sort of thing. The second, community accompaniment, helps guide people to move past the agency mentality into the L'Arche way of being, to learn to live in community, to build relationships, to meet people in terms of who they are rather than in terms of what they have to contribute to our own agendas or what they demand from us.

The third kind of accompaniment that all assistants receive is spiritual accompaniment on their personal journeys. This, obviously, isn't something that a stranger passing through for a day can start interrogating her hosts about, regardless of their IQ. But the emotional and spiritual aspects of L'Arche are something that Vanier writes about a good deal. People with disabilities often suffer acutely from the pain of strangeness, rejection, guilt. Vanier has many stories to tell of individuals who have arrived at L'Arche communities from institutions in a condition of anguish that expresses itself in violent and disruptive behavior and who gradually, as they live in a community that sees them not merely as problems to be dealt with but as people to be loved in their weakness, learn to trust and to find peace and joy. And this experience of transformation extends to the assistants who come to L'Arche from the competitive, thrusting world.

Life in a community in which relationships transcend the "us" and "them" division of "normal" and "disabled" reveals deep truths about humanity. We all, Vanier says, carry with us a hunger for belonging and unconditional love, a pain of inner solitude, a "wound of loneliness."[15] The situation is exacerbated in highly mobile, competitive, individualistic Western societies that encourage us to cover over and forget the wound and go in search of goals—wealth, success, efficiency, control—which have the

15. Vanier, *Community and Growth*, 327.

approval of culture but which can never meet our needs. Mme. Verdurin looks for security and fulfillment in social success and admiration, and Casaubon in intellectual achievement; both are still haunted by the fear of inadequacy and failure that drives them deeper into egotism and isolation. Journey's neighbors put up a tall fence to protect their vision of suburban normality from the disturbing specter of vulnerability and weakness. Anybody who crosses the threshold of a L'Arche house, whether core members, assistants, or nosey overnight visitors, bring with them their own wounds and their own habits of concealment and denial. The experience of L'Arche, as Vanier understands it, is a sign of our need for both community and relationship. "Community is the place where our limitations, our fears and our egoism are revealed to us," he writes.

> While we are alone, we could believe that we loved everyone. Now that we are with others . . . we realize how incapable we are of loving, how much we deny to others, how closed in on ourselves we are . . . Community life with all its pain is the revelation of a terrible wound.[16]

Community forces "normal" people, people with the resources to "succeed" in the terms dictated by the prevalent culture, to confront the knowledge of their own incompleteness, which those who are obviously strangers—the poor, the homeless, the handicapped—cannot avoid. At the same time it offers the possibility of healing.

> As all the inner pains surface, we can discover too that community is a safe place. At last some people really listen to us; we can, little by little, reveal to them all those terrible monsters within us . . . and they can help us to accept them by revealing to us that these monsters are protecting our vulnerability and are our cry for and our fear of love. They stand at the door of our wounded heart.[17]

16. Ibid., 26–27
17. Ibid., 27

Life in community is a means both to respond to the challenge of the Gospel by meeting the needs of strangers, and to come to terms with the universal reality of estrangement and vulnerability. The "wound of loneliness" cannot be fully healed—Dorothy Day, who wrote that "we are as crowded as the poor are, with people sleeping in every available corner,"[18] called her autobiography *The Long Loneliness*—because it is a longing for the infinite. But, according to Vanier, if loneliness is acknowledged, "it can become the place of meeting with God, and with brothers and sisters; it can become the place . . . of the eternal wedding feast."[19]

The vision of community, of welcome, of humanity that is embodied in the L'Arche and in the Catholic Worker is radical, deeply so. Surely, for someone to leave a middle-class life of conventional achievement to share the life of those made strangers by poverty or disability is not the gracious balance that I have called welcome, but rather a form of surrender to the other more extreme than Lydgate's, or Moshe and Malli's. To some extent, it absolutely is. And, as we will see in the next chapter, the closer we draw to God, to seeing the stranger not as a fellow human being but as Christ himself, the closer we will be drawn to the ultimate necessity of absolute surrender.

Certainly these communities involve immense sacrifice; a great deal that most of us take for granted has to be given up—security, privacy, comfort, autonomy, the company of one's peers. But they are also a sign—and herein lies what Pohl calls the social transformative power of hospitality—that security, privacy, and autonomy are not, in the end, essential to human happiness or integrity, and that to believe they are is to be taken in by a vision of life that comes not from the Gospel but from the world, a vision marked by suspicion and greed and competition and selfishness and hostility and prejudice and fear, a vision that, despite its own claim to being final, despite its stranglehold on our society, *can* be resisted and rejected. Voluntary

18. Day, *House of Hospitality*, 130.
19. Vanier, *Community and Growth*, 28.

poverty in the Catholic Worker tradition rejects the prevailing idea that human integrity requires tidiness, decorum, security, homogeneity, some approximation to bourgeois life. It walks, eyes open, into a life marked by poverty and creates there new patterns whose integrity and dignity cannot be shattered by dirt and disorder. Community as lived by L'Arche challenges our assumptions about what makes a human life valuable, what makes a human person worthy of love, what it means to enter into a relationship, to be a friend. Life in these communities exposes the society around us as obsessively grasping and controlling and creates a different society in which personal wholeness can be discovered free from the distortions of a commercial culture, and the balance of welcome can be relearned.

Or that's what I think. My own timid experience with hospitality, of course, barely merits the name compared to the radical, selfless generosity of the Catholic Worker and L'Arche, but it has given me a glimpse of the kind of transformation that welcome and community can make possible. The people whom Glen and I try to welcome are bright, interested, likeable. That they decide to make themselves at home with us, show up at odd hours with new friends or broken hearts, treat us to interminable tales of late-adolescent drama or dreadful movies, keep us up half the night, show up at dinnertime three nights a week or decide that our kitchen is the best place to make sushi or cupcakes, feels to me like a huge privilege. And it is loads of fun. But lots of our grown-up friends—not mean-spirited, uptight neat freaks, but warm, generous, Christian people, colleagues who are thoroughly committed to the welfare of students—think we are nuts and wonder how and why we put up with it.

The difference between my own delight at being so warmly taken for granted and my friends' bewilderment as to why on earth we live like this is in part simply a matter of taste and temperament. It also shows, however, that one's sense of the normal and the needful can be altered by experience and habit. To many of our friends, a fairly high degree of privacy and productivity and order seems both normal and necessary for proper adult life. I am used to having rather less of these than most of the people we know, and I find I do perfectly well without them. On the other hand I have plenty of expectations about the normal and the necessary. I take it for granted that we have a bedroom and a bank account to ourselves. I take it for granted that none of the people who drop in when they feel like it is going to bring drugs into the house, get into fistfights, or ask us to raise bail money. I take it for granted that none of the people who have occupied the spare room over the years has needed my help in the bathroom, taken an hour to clear the table, or communicated only in squawks. But if I were to step out into the footsteps of Dorothy Day or Jean Vanier, become part of a community that is designed around welcoming those most estranged from our society, then I suppose—I suppose—that this would change, that my demands for control would relax, that my egotistical, fearful need for a normality built in my own image would loosen, that my view of humanity would broaden, that my ability to welcome and love would deepen. My day with the people at Journey gave me just a faint glimpse of how this might happen and what it might mean.

The work and writings of Day and Vanier make clear that the "socially transformative potential of hospitality"—its power to create new kinds of relationships between strangers—cannot be separated from its spiritually transformative potential—its power to change those things in us that cling to or refuse relationships. This is both the challenge and the promise of the biblical stories of welcome—Abraham at Mamre, the sheep and the goats—and of the ventures that spring from them. With every relationship we embrace or refuse, every stranger we welcome or avoid, we shape both the world around us and the soul that will one day encounter, face to face, the one who has, all along, been every stranger.

5

Love Bade Me Welcome

Hospitality and the Spirit

We began the first chapter by glancing briefly at the story of Abraham who, in welcoming strangers, welcomed God and entered into covenant with him. From there we turned to a more modest, more familiar kind of hospitality, the kind exercised in modern Western households—the Verdurins, Martine and Philippa, Moshe and Malli—and since then we have moved outwards, from the relatively simple transactions of domestic hospitality, to the richer, more complex and demanding bond of marriage, to the realm of ideas, to pressing questions of social justice and Christian responsibility. At all of these levels a central theme has been that of balance; I have maintained that the fruitfulness of true welcome is found in a graced and disciplined poise between the extremes of egotistical control over others, and abject surrender of self. But fallen, wounded, human nature is off-balance: we veer between neediness and brutality, from tenderness to compulsion, perpetually colliding with or clutching at each other, desperately or violently, in ignorance or desire or fear. The practice of hospitality, as we have seen, can be a school of self-knowledge, of honesty, of humility, and thus of equilibrium, of stability. Stability, in its turn, makes possible real welcome: of the refugee, of the poor or handicapped, of the stranger.

This brings us back to the place we started from: to Abraham welcoming God in the person of the three strangers. What this story hints at, and what the parable of the sheep and goats makes explicit, is that every encounter with a stranger is an encounter with God. And here, suddenly, all bets are off and the delicate art of balance and welcome is irrelevant. The first and the final encounter of our human experience is with one who has entered into our human experience of vulnerability, but not into that of teetering, precarious instability. The stranger we welcomed or rejected is the great I AM, the still point of the turning world, the ground of all being, the Son of Man who welcomes the sheep into his kingdom and sends the goats away. The work, the sacrifice, the mess, the risk of learning to be a host, turns out to be merely a preparation for the final vocation of being a guest. And that, it turns out, is much harder.

In Luke 14 Jesus, on his final journey from Galilee to Jerusalem, goes to eat the Sabbath meal at the house of the local Pharisee. His relationship with the Pharisees is pretty tense by this time. He draws crowds that have long since outgrown the synagogues, and the Pharisees are both jealous of his popularity and suspicious of his cavalier approach to the law. Jesus, for his part, isn't afraid of being confrontational: he is sometimes sarcastic, sometimes openly critical of their warped motivation and their self-serving hypocrisy. Despite the tensions, however, Jesus is an important figure in their world, or the world that they think of as theirs, and when he passes through a town, he is typically invited over by the Pharisee. On this occasion, Jesus watches while other guests "choose the places of honor." "When you are invited by someone to a wedding banquet," he advises them, "do not sit down at the place of honor," because the host might move you down, embarrassingly, to make room for someone of higher status. Instead, he recommends sitting at a lower place "so that when your host comes he may say to you, 'Friend, move up higher'; then you will be honored in the presence of all who sit at the table with you."

The guests' behavior is immediately familiar; they are motivated by hunger for status, by the desire to be, or to appear, well-connected, to be able to drop into conversation, with studied nonchalance, "You know it's funny you should say that, because just last week I was at dinner with [insert name guaranteed to impress or intimidate] and *he* said . . ." It's the age-old game of networking, influence peddling, social climbing, and ego bolstering: precisely what the Verdurins are all about. We all do it in our own way, and we hope that nobody will notice, but of course Jesus does and calls them out on it, pointing out that social climbing is a dangerous sport, as likely to end in bruising humiliation as in elevation.

After showing up the self-serving behavior of his fellow guests, Jesus moves on to implicitly criticizing his host for inviting them in the first place: the Pharisees seem to have taken on the pagan model of hospitality as a means of making and cementing social relations that appear advantageous but that are in reality superficial and transitory. When you have people over for a meal, Jesus says, you should not invite people who will invite you back, but instead, welcome those who have nothing to offer in return. "And you will be blessed, because they cannot repay you, for you will be repaid at the resurrection of the righteous."

This is no way to behave at a dinner party, even a religious one; everyone probably feels awkward and embarrassed by now. Someone says, "Blessed is he who will eat bread in the kingdom of God," hoping that everybody will agree on this pious platitude, and the conversation can move back to safer terrain. But again, Jesus isn't playing. He turns his attention back to the role of the guest and tells the story of a certain man who holds a "great dinner." On the day of the party, he sends out servants to remind his guests that it was time to come.

But they don't come. Every last one sends his excuses and regrets. The host sends his servant back out, this time to the park benches and back alleys, to bring in the kind of people who don't normally get invited to dinner parties, let alone great feasts: the kind of people you're more likely to meet in a Catholic Worker or L'Arche house. Of those originally invited, the host declares, none will taste a bite of the supper. Blessed is he who will eat bread in the kingdom of God? Surely. But not everyone will, Jesus implies. And as some will be shut out, according to Matthew 25, because they had seen the Son of Man as a stranger and had not taken him in, so will some simply because they turned down an invitation to blessedness. Our relationship with God, the story suggests, hangs on how we behave as guests, as well as on how we behave as hosts.

Why would anyone turn down God's welcome, his invitation into blessedness? For the same reasons, it would seem, as they turn down invitations to parties. So why is *that*? What makes people hesitant to accept hospitality? This question and the story that it arises from make me uncomfortable because it is a hesitancy I know myself. I am entirely happy to be taken for granted by hordes of importunate hungry youngsters. I love when people come to stay and are packed into the house like sardines and there's eighteen of them at breakfast eating pancakes in shifts. But I'm not as comfortable as a guest. I much prefer hospitality to happen on my own turf, with me as host, although I have to do the shopping and cooking beforehand, and deal with the wreckage afterwards. Why?

I want to look at three ways of answering this question. The first kind of answer is that given by the guests in Jesus' story. They cannot come—"cannot" rather than "will not," they say—because they are busy. One is recently married, one has just bought land, one has bought oxen; they have to—"have to," they say, not "want to" or "prefer to"—to see to their affairs. They have places to go, people to see, things to accomplish that take precedence over the supper. The appeal to busyness is such a common one in our culture that it seems quite straightforward and innocent. But it has a sinister edge. Their indifference to anything going on outside the immediate sphere of their personal concerns is surely not too far from the indifference of Matthew's "goats" to the needs of the stranger. This indifference grows from unthinking conformity to the world and from a habit of self-absorption so deeply rooted that it keeps them from seeing that they are making a choice, let alone the implications of that choice.

For a second perspective—in some regards entirely different—on the question of why people reject an offer of welcome, we can turn to George Herbert's beautiful poem "Love," in which the encounter between God and the soul is put as a dialogue between a host and a guest.

> Love bade me welcome; but my soul drew back,
> > Guilty of dust and sin
> But quick-eyed love, observing me grow slack
> > From my first entrance in,
> Drew nearer to me, sweetly questioning
> > If I lack'd anything.
>
> "A guest," I answer'd, "worthy to be here."
> > Love said, "You shall be he."
> "I, the unkind, ungrateful? Ah, my dear,
> > I cannot look on thee."
> Love took my hand and smiling did reply,
> > "Who made those eyes but I?"
>
> "Truth, Lord; but I have marr'd them: let my shame
> > Go where it doth deserve."
> "And know you not," says Love, "who bore the blame?"
> > "My dear, then I will serve."
> "You must sit down," says Love, "and taste my meat."
> > So I did sit and eat.

The guest is hesitant to enter the house, to look his host in the eye, to sit at his table, because he knows he does not deserve to be there. He is tainted by "dust and sin," he is "unkind, ungrateful," and he has misused and "marred" his own nature, which is in itself a gift from his host. This is not false modesty, or conventional demurring—"oh, that's so kind of you but I don't want to put you to the trouble"—but the simple truth. Love, the host, does not argue with him, "Oh no, it's no trouble at all, we'd be delighted to have you." He tacitly acknowledges everything the guest says, and moves past it. He created his guest's very nature; when that nature was soiled by "dust and sin," he "bore the blame"; and now, he insists, he will continue to play what is in fact the primary role in the relationship, the role of service.

We can find the same pattern in the gospels. When Peter meets Jesus, his first response is to recoil, protesting, "Go away from me, Lord, for I am a sinful man!" (Luke 5:8). Jesus doesn't argue with him; he just ignores his protest and tells him not to be afraid but to come with him, and Peter leaves everything and follows. The same thing happens at their last encounter, before Jesus' death: Peter insists that Jesus must not humble himself to wash Peter's feet, and Jesus pushes past his objections and washes them. Here, as in Herbert's poem, unwillingness to accept welcome is born of shame and is overridden by the gentle, unyielding persistence of love.

A third account of why people turn away from welcome, even when they understand what is at stake, is suggested in C. S. Lewis' wonderful book *The Great Divorce*—an extended, fantastical, sometimes chilling riff on the story Jesus tells the Pharisees. The novel opens when the narrator finds himself in an endless dusk, in a dreary town that extends itself to infinity, inhabited by querulous and isolated people who are haunted by some undefined sense of threat as to what will happen when night finally comes. He joins a line waiting for a bus that rises into the air and takes them to a place bounded in the distance by towering mountains, a place on the brink of dawn, so fresh and open that "it made the Solar System itself seem an indoor affair," and so solid and substantial that the humans getting off the bus are revealed to be ghosts—transparent, "man-shaped stains on the brightness of the air"—unable so much as to pick up the fruit of the country or to crush the grass, which is as painfully unyielding as diamonds under their feet.[1] From the mountains come Bright People, the true inhabitants of the place, as solid and as beautiful as the land around them.

The heart of the book is a series of dialogues that the narrator observes. Each of the Bright People, like the servant sent out in Luke 14 to bring in the guests, has come to meet a ghost with whom they had a connection in life and to persuade them to stay and to come with them to the mountains. With one exception all of the ghosts, receiving an invitation to bliss, reject it, and make their way back to the bus, which is waiting to take them to the dingy endless town and the threat of darkness that hovers over it. In the abstract, the choice is incomprehensible. Lewis, however, makes each individual particular ghost's choice unnervingly understandable, giving a glimpse of a life made up of a succession of choices that all culminate, eerily, in the choice against joy.

The first dialogue sets the pattern for the others. The Big Ghost is approached by a Bright Spirit—Len—who, the reader learns, was his employee, and who had murdered a mutual acquaintance of theirs and, like Herbert's guest, had been led through shame to self-forgetfulness: "I have given up myself," he tells the Big Ghost. "I had to, you know, after the murder. That is what it did for me. And that is how everything began."[2] He urges his companion to come with him, but the Big Ghost is appalled and offended by this reversal in their situation, which appears to him as a bitter injustice. To accept Len's help and guidance would be to abandon the myth of decency and self-sufficiency that he has constructed around his own character. "Look at me, now," he insists.

> "I gone straight all my life. I don't say I was a religious man and I don't say I had no faults, far from it. But I done my best all my life, see? I done my best by everyone, that's the sort of chap I was. I never asked for

1. Lewis, *Great Divorce*, 28.
2. Ibid., 34.

> anything that wasn't mine by rights. If I wanted a drink
> I paid for it and if I took my wages I done my job, see?
> That's the sort I was and I don't care who knows it."[3]

Len tries to divert him. "It would be much better not to go on about that now," he says. "Only be happy and come with me." But the Big Ghost keeps insisting: "I only want my rights. I'm not asking for anybody's bleeding charity." Len responds, "Then do. At once. Ask for the Bleeding Charity. Everything is here for the asking and nothing can be bought."[4]

Len, like Herbert's "Love," tries to shift the subject from the particular story of the individual to the universality of grace, but the Big Ghost's insistence on his own righteousness keeps him from hearing and accepting the Spirit's offer, and in the end he makes an explicit choice, only half-disguising its implications from himself under casual profanity.

> It had been entreated: it could make a refusal; and this
> seemed to it a kind of advantage . . . "I'm not coming,
> see? I'd rather be damned than go along with you."[5]

The Big Ghost's defining characteristic is pride—the root of all sins—in a very simple form, naked and unsophisticated. In later dialogues, Lewis shows us subtler variations on the same theme from ghosts who nuance their motives more finely. Some are like the guests in Luke 14, concerned with trivial business that blinds them to the solemn significance of their situation. One ghost ignores the glory all around him, and concentrates all his energies on the pathetic attempt to bring a tiny but immensely heavy apple back on the bus to the ghostly town to sell as a commodity. A bishop who, in search of earthly prestige, had given himself over to fashionable liberal theology and allowed his faith to be eroded, declines the invitation to meet God face to face because of his engagement to deliver a talk at a theological society

3. Ibid., 27.
4. Ibid., 34.
5. Ibid., 36.

in the town. One woman is like the guest in Herbert's poem: crippled by shame, painfully aware of her own transparency, of her unfitness for the country. "How can I go out like this among a lot of people with real solid bodies? It's far worse than going out with nothing on would have been on earth."[6]

Other dialogues are darker. The ghost called Pam has lost a son. Although the Spirit of her brother tells her that Michael is waiting for her in the mountains, she will not go with him, prevented by her rage at the cruelty of her loss, made self-righteous by the idol she has constructed of her grief. The Hard-Bitten Ghost has schooled himself to resist disappointment by trusting nothing but his own shrewd worldly cynicism. He fools himself that he is not really rejecting an offer by insisting that the welcome and promise of the country is not what it seems. The dwarfish ghost called Frank, implored to enter into joy by the saintly Spirit who was once his wife, refuses to let go of the lifelong habit of manipulating others, a habit so well established that it has taken the form of a separate being: a seedy Tragedian who towers over the real man and eventually consumes him altogether.

Bewildered and distressed by these conversations, and deeply uneasy himself in the hard country, the narrator comes across a Spirit who explains to him the significance of the conversations, and the nature of the choice that all of the ghosts—all human souls—face. The Spirit tells him, "There are only two kinds of people in the end: those who say to God, 'Thy will be done,' and those to whom God says, in the end, 'Thy will be done.' All that are in Hell, choose it."[7] Nothing is keeping these souls from joy except for their own refusal to accept it, to be guests. Each insists on being the protagonist of the story, on making their personal achievement or sorrow or anger or desire the motivation of the crucial choice and action. What that story is, what the nature of the choice, the consequences of the action, matters less to them

6. Ibid., 61.
7. Ibid., 69.

than that it be theirs personally, that it begin and end with them, that it find its meaning in reference to themselves.

Seen in this light, then, all reasons for which people reject the hospitality of others are manifestations of the same basic human orientation. For the guests in Jesus' story their own private affairs are of greater moment than anybody else's; what their excuses really say is that they are unwilling to step out of the role of protagonist of their own busyness, even for an evening, to play the bit part of guest in the story of someone else's party. The guest in Herbert's poem, until he is overborne by Love's perseverance, insists on seeing his own unworthiness, guilt, dustiness, rather than the host's welcome, as the most important element of the relationship. Worldly busyness is not an innocent fact of life, and shame is not so much the opposite of pride as its close cousin inasmuch as they both insist on their own centrality.

All of these unwilling guests have this in common with those bad hosts we have seen, those who seek to control, to force or manipulate the world around them into a pattern of their own creation; like Dawkins and Shaeffer, like Rosamund, like Mme. Verdurin they are motivated, in the end, by fear. As Christmas approaches, Mme. Verdurin becomes tense and shrill, gripped by the terror that her usual guests will be claimed by family commitments and will deprive her of her role as host, leaving her alone with herself. Like her these other unwilling guests are afraid of being forced to confront their own final vulnerability and dependence, and cling to familiar and hollow patterns of self-description and self-understanding. This is true even of the most seemingly innocent of excuses. The ubiquitous appeal to the overcrowded schedule—"Oh thanks, we'd love to, but this week is really nuts. Let me look at my calendar and get back to you, okay?"—may be quite sincere. Our schedules may indeed be overcrowded, but why do we let them get that way? Don't we brandish the loaded calendar as a shield to hide from ourselves and others our vulnerability, our contingency, by maintaining an illusion of control? I am pretty sure that I do. I am rarely so busy that I will not cheerfully rearrange things when people come round, but when I'm invited out I often feel crowded and pressured, acutely aware of how much I have to do. I suspect that it's not really about time at all: it's that I, like Mme. Verdurin, am only really comfortable in a space ordered around my own personality. This is a dangerous business. The kingdom of Heaven will not be ordered that way.

The overcrowded schedule may be a modern phenomenon, but the collusion of pride, fear, and shame against an offer of hospitality is an old story: the very oldest, in fact. We can read the story of the fall as a rejection of hospitality. The garden is God's, and Adam and Eve are his guests, lovingly ushered into being and generously provided for by a host who anticipates their every need. In this reading the presence of the forbidden fruit represents the integrity and priority of God's nature: all other natures are always guests of his grace and never absolute possessors of their own being. But the man and woman reject this arrangement, refuse to be guests, to live in a world and in bodies and minds created for their delight and put at their disposal. They insist on being sole proprietors, lords of the universe, and we follow in their footsteps, struggling to enthrone our tiny, contingent egos at the center of existence.

Of course it doesn't work. As soon as their eyes are opened, the first thing Adam and Eve see is that they are naked, vulnerable, and they reach for leaves to cover themselves. This is the deepest effect of pride: it plunges us into shame at the secret knowledge of our own smallness and, deeper, into fear. Once we have committed ourselves to the lie of our own self-sufficiency, our possession of ourselves and our world, trust is replaced by suspicion, and we are dominated by the terrified need to protect ourselves from exposure and from the competing claims of the billions of others in the same predicament as ourselves. Unless something greater frees us into humility and truth, the fear into which pride plunges us dominates our lives, and the goods of the created world—our neighbors, our words, our religions, the very leaves on the trees—become objects to us, fodder for our frantic and destructive attempts to sustain, for others and our selves, the desperate illusion that we are gods, rather than the guests of Love who waits to welcome, serve, and feed us.

This may seem like a hopelessly self-serving, idiosyncratic interpretation of the story. Perhaps it is; most certainly it is partial. But a few chapters after Jesus tells the story of the great dinner, he tells another story that pulls in this direction, to an audience considerably more hostile and dangerous than the Pharisees. In Luke 20, Jesus has arrived in Jerusalem, cleared out the merchants in the temple, and established himself there. The priests and the temple authorities are appalled. They want to kill him but are kept from acting by the crowds of common people who love Jesus and flock to him, so instead they lurk around, and try crudely to trick him into saying something that will give them a chance to get rid of him. He brushes them off and turns back to the crowd to whom he tells the story of tenants in a vineyard, who beat up and send away the servants that the owner sends to collect the rent. Eventually the owner has to send his son; the tenants see him coming, and decide to kill him, telling themselves that then they will be able to take the vineyard for their own, and not have to worry about the owner or the rent anymore. They have to know that it won't work that way, but they persuade themselves otherwise.

There are a number of things going on as Jesus tells his story. Firstly, he is letting the priests know that he is on to them. He knows their plans, but makes no attempt to placate or evade them. His calm certainty of their schemes must in itself be rather unnerving. More disturbing still is the light the story casts on his enemies' motivation. In effect, he is saying to the priests, "You have been put in charge of God's temple, God's people. Your livelihood, your status, your power all come from what God has entrusted you with. You are his guests. But you'd prefer to forget that. You'd prefer that this place belong to you. And at bottom you hate God, don't you? You resent him; you wish he didn't exist, that he wouldn't hold you accountable, that you were really the masters. Do you really imagine that it's going to work? Oh, sure, you'll kill me, I know *that*. But you can't actually think that God will fade into the scenery and leave this place and this people in your hands?" To have one's secret thoughts laid bare like this is no less shaming than to have one's naked body exposed; small wonder that the priests' resolve to get rid of him is redoubled.

The priests' murderous rage at Jesus springs from the fact that they had usurped his Father's house. Perhaps, like them, when we are uncomfortable about being guests, it is in part because we are uncomfortable about the fact that we are already guests, and bad ones. We are squatters in a house that belongs to someone else. And we have trashed the place—there are broken windows, carpets soaked in beer (and worse), fights in the yard, drug deals in the bathroom. We're not too far gone to realize we've made a squalid mess of a beautiful house, nor to understand that, despite occasional brief forays with a trash bag and a broom, we are not in a position to fix it; we simply don't have the resources. If the mess is ever to be cleaned up and the house restored to its original condition, the owner is going to have to do it, and heaven only knows what it's going to cost him. We can't bear to think about it, so we pretend it isn't happening and go on living as if this is our house and the mess affects nobody but ourselves. Like Lewis's ghosts we are burdened, enchained to misery by the weight of habit. We are frightened by the knowledge of what we deserve from the owner, but, like Herbert's guest, we are still more frightened by the notion that he might want to welcome us, love us, care for us, clean us, forgive us, feed us.

This is our predicament, then, and this is where the two sides of hospitality—the role of host and that of guest—meet. The first role can train us for the second. Peter, called by Jesus, simply walked away from his nets and his home and his shame, and followed him. Most of us can't. Being a guest requires us to be weightless; to leave behind our tangled stories, our human baggage, the sorrow and business and self-importance and anger and shame and cynicism that we clutch to ourselves, the clutter that we use to define and protect us. As Lewis says, "You cannot take all luggage with you on all journeys; on one journey even your right hand and your right eye may be among the things you have to leave behind," and simply abandoning it, giving up our burdens, our illusions of control—our *selves*—is more than most of us can face.[8] But being a host can help prepare us. If we cultivate the practice of hospitality, if we learn to welcome, we learn to balance the baggage of our lives, to loosen our grip on it and lessen its grip on us. When we share with others the things that are, at least superficially, ours—our space, our food, our recognition, our attention—those things become lighter.

My own forays into hospitality in the footsteps of Joe and Linette have taught me, among other things, that I don't need to exert absolute control over my own schedule, that I can live with uncertainty about who will show up at dinnertime, or at eleven at night. It's a pain in the neck sometimes, but I've no doubt that I'm a happier person for it. Those like Day and Vanier and their heirs who go much further down the path, learn to let go of more and become, correspondingly, lighter, aware of their own vulnerabilities, more able to carry their burden with poise and grace, and more ready to accept the hospitality that they have sacrificially given to others. The journey of learning to welcome is central to the Christian vocation but is provisional, a preparation for the final journey of accepting welcome. The roles of guest and host are both of spiritual significance; perhaps both those who come to us in need of hospitality and those who offer us hospitality will be revealed to be the Son of Man.

This is what Martine and Philippa find. Their relationship with the refugee whom they had taken into their home is fulfilled only when their roles are reversed and they become guests at her feast. The sisters find it difficult: for all their awareness of Babette's difference, for all the grace and poise with which they have welcomed her into their life while respecting her privacy,

8. Ibid., 9.

they still find security in their roles as hosts. Becoming guests, relinquishing control over the ordered habits of their household causes them intense anxiety, and they are inclined to refuse. But they cannot deny the force of her plea: "Had she ever, during twelve years, asked a favor?" she asks, and it is a rhetorical question; they all know the answer: "No! . . . Babette was right; it was her first request these twelve years."

It is an odd exchange. Since the night when she arrived, storm-tossed and desperate, a stranger at their door, Babette has been entirely dependent on the sisters and on the ascetic piety that has schooled them in hospitality and charity. What right has she to claim that she has never asked anything from them? Yet the sisters understand. By accepting *her* hospitality, by becoming her guests, by placing themselves within the perilous gravitational pull of her alien world, they are acknowledging the humanity that they have respected, but have never fully encountered. In doing so they become, for the first time, the "good people" she had come to Norway to find. And in eating Babette's feast, their querulous, repressed community rediscover the love at the foundation of the Brotherhood and the meaning of the texts that had become stale formulas. Mercy and truth *do* meet together, righteousness and peace *do* kiss one another as the Brotherhood eat Babette's food.

The true significance of Babette's feast (or "great dinner") is revealed only after it is over. "We will remember this evening when you have gone back to Paris, Babette," Martine tells her after the guests have left. Martine and Philippa had thought of the evening with sorrow, as a farewell to the stranger whom they had sheltered, and whom the lottery money had lifted out of their sphere and back into her own. When it is ended and they are alone with Babette, they learn that instead the great dinner was not a farewell but, in a sense, a wedding banquet, marking the sealing of a permanent bond. Babette tells the bewildered sisters that she is not going back to Paris. Not only are all the people who gave meaning to her life there now gone, she tells them, but she has no money: she has spent all her winnings on the meal and is as poor as they are. Babette has poured herself out; while they were eating her food they were consuming everything that separated her from them. In giving all she had to feed the community, she has both united herself forever with the narrow world that had welcomed her and has drawn it up into the world of delight that she came from. The stranger whom the sisters welcomed, out of obedience to the gospel, is revealed to be one who has poured herself out to bring life to their world.

We can, perhaps, read the entire story of salvation history as an exchange of hospitality. We rejected God's welcome: we refused to be his guests in Eden and exiled ourselves to a wilderness of shame and hostility and fear. God did not abandon us. He came to us in our exile, condescending to be our guest in the world that we had seized as our own. He humbled himself to accept the hospitality of a woman's body, emptied himself to enter into our life in space and time and history, into a body vulnerable to hunger and exhaustion and the violence that springs from greed and pride and fear. In the end he entered into the grave and, here, comes into his kingdom and offers us welcome, into his Father's house, into his wedding banquet, into a new heaven and a new earth, and into his own nature. Now he offers himself again as our guest, so that we can learn to be his.

Epilogue

To Care and Not to Care

When I started writing this book, about a year ago, Robby and his guitar were here all the time. Now he's got a girlfriend and we hardly ever see him and the Thursday night movie group, which for a while had expanded into a rolling jam session, has morphed back into a group that meets on Thursday nights to watch movies. It's a good thing—with Robby permanently installed I would have learned a lot more songs, but I would have written rather less of this book. And while I think it was good for him to hang out here for a bit while he was sorting out a few things, he's sorted them out and it was time for him to move on. But we do miss his flat-footed stomp coming up the front steps, his goofy guileless honesty, and his music.

This, of course, is the way it goes; students move in, move through and move on. Some of the students we've been close to over the years are among our best friends; we stay in close touch, plan our summers around each other, and travel cross-country to meet each others' new babies. We might still be friends with Robby in ten years: that would be lovely. But most we hear from rarely, or have lost track of altogether. Some, of course, graduate, move away, and leave college behind; others, while they are still here, simply close the chapter in their life of which we were part.

Robby may or may not remember to come say goodbye when he graduates.

If he doesn't, I admit I'll be sad. But that will be entirely my problem: heaven forbid that he should so much as suspect it. Being outgrown, gradually or abruptly, is part of what we sign on for when we open the doors. The friendships we have with students are real and rewarding, and sometimes deep, and they may evolve over time into grown-up relationships between equals, but while the students are students the relationships are asymmetrical, and if they are to be healthy and balanced they have to be built around that asymmetry. We have responsibilities to the kids who congregate here; they, beyond the obligations of basic courtesy, have none to us. They set the boundaries where it suits them; we patrol them. They assign us a role in the current phase of their lives; we play it. We are mature enough, our lives have enough stability, to accommodate a variety of roles. Within reason, of course, we can be all things to all people, and over the years we've gotten pretty good at figuring out what people we can most usefully be what things to. We make available ourselves, our house, our affection for them, and what wisdom about life we have acquired, but it is up to them to determine what use, if any, they want to make of it and for how long. It would be way out of line for us to try to impose our middle-aged stability on the changeability of people at a different stage in life.

It's not easy. I am, as I had said, temperamentally far too much like Mme. Verdurin for my own comfort, and fading uncomplainingly into the background does not come naturally; I'm much more inclined to cling and sulk. I did, once; I messed up very badly, and was saved from the results of it only by the most extraordinary instance of grace that I have known. Lara and Gabe were both remarkable people. She is enchanting: sharp intelligence and waifish beauty, insight and honesty, curiosity and compassion. He is possibly the smartest person I know and has a capacity for stoical self-denial that bewilders everybody who knows him. They both also had terribly difficult backgrounds—poverty, addiction, abuse, a litany of all the things that drag young lives down into chaos. They had stumbled into each other among the darkness and had a child together; when we met them, Spencer was two and they were barely out of their teens. For all their gifts, the odds were heavily stacked against them, and for most of the three years they lived near us they were separated and lurching through a series of crises. We became particularly close to Gabe who, for a while, was essentially raising Spencer alone; our eldest, who was just emerging from babyhood, loved Spence fiercely. Then Lara hit a crisis so severe that even she couldn't bluff her way through. She moved back in with Gabe and Spence, determined that although they hadn't been her first priority, they might be her last hope. They closed ranks, and Gabe and Spencer, whom we had seen almost every day for over a year, stopped coming round.

I don't know if Mme. Verdurin herself would have handled it much worse than I did. I lost my balance thoroughly. There was nothing wrong with my feeling sad: I had every right to miss them, and my daughter cried for Spencer every day for months. But I didn't just feel sad. I felt bitter and angry and betrayed and mistrustful and jealous and fearful. It wasn't pretty. I made a feeble attempt to hide it all behind a mask of mature concern and friendly support and fought to keep a place in their lives, but Lara, for all she was a mess at the time, was no fool and was having none of it. She told me to back off, with such ferocity that I didn't dare protest further, and I slunk off to lick my wounds, my concern over what would become of them almost lost among my anxiety over what I would do with myself without them to look after.

Through mutual friends, bits of news trickled in from time to time—they had graduated, moved away, started grad school, got married, had another baby. The news was all good, very good indeed, far better than we would have dared to hope, and our concern waned, but for a long time I was still selfishly tangled up in the utterly trivial fact of my own rejection. I made periodic attempts to write to them, but I would look over the letter and know that it was insincere, informed by my own need and would never get past Lara's radar for emotional bullshit. It was fully four years before I produced a letter, ruthlessly pruned, scrutinized for any trace of manipulation and pruned again, saying in as few words as possible that we had heard they were doing well, that we were happy for them, and that we sent our best wishes. I sent it off, and tried to let go.

Almost immediately a letter of astonishing grace arrived from Lara—it still lives in a drawer by my bed where I consult it when I need reassurance that God is bigger than our faults. A couple of weeks later they came to visit. Lara, now properly in command of the gifts that had previously served her as a life raft, dissolved all awkwardness before they were fairly in the door, the conversation with the imperturbable Gabe took up more or less in mid-sentence, and my children practically devoured Spencer— now a fabulously cool skateboarding big kid—and his baby sister. We see them whenever we can manage it; it's an eight-hour drive to their teeny house where we sleep in a basement that smells of cat, but it's so totally worth it. There are four children now with all the talents of their parents and a wonderfully warm, creative, secure home to develop them in. It took me a while to get used to not worrying about them anymore, but I hope I will never get over the joy and gratitude that fills me whenever I think of them.

The story has a happy outcome for all of us, but I hope I haven't let that make me complacent about my own part in it: I learned, painfully, just how far astray my tendency to control and cling can lead me. I have taken the lesson to heart and have been scrupulously careful since then to keep my balance and make sure that I don't expect college kids to bear the burden of my own self-image. Here, too, Joe and Linette are inspirations. I'm sure I was not the only one who thought, hours after arriving for the first visit, "Okay, that's it. This is who I want to be when I grow up," but they seemed serenely indifferent to our gratitude, affection, and admiration, and any attempts to try to build a cult of personality around them would, I imagine, have been brushed off rather abruptly. Whether or not it required conscious effort on their part, as it does on mine, I don't know, but that's precisely the point; their house, their food, their time was at our disposal, but their business was theirs alone.

But Joe and Linette are real people and, being the huge nerd that I am, I never quite feel sure of anything until I have found it in a novel. Mme. Verdurin is an ever-present and invaluable warning against egotism and control, but as a positive example I need someone a bit more specific to my situation than the pious Norwegian spinsters, and I find it in Cara, a minor character in Evelyn Waugh's *Brideshead Revisited*. During a vacation from university (by a happy symmetry, Oxford), Charles, the novel's narrator, accompanies his friend Sebastian to Venice where Sebastian's father, the apostate Lord Marchmain, lives with his mistress. Charles, already bewitched by the charm of his aristocratic friend, is overwhelmed by the majesty of Venice. "I was drowning in honey, stingless," he says.[1]

But Cara has been watching the young men closely and knows that there are stings invisible to the enchanted Charles: things that he does not have the maturity to see or understand. When they happen to find themselves alone, she opens a conversation that he remembers for many years. In Cara's place I would probably begin with a fanfare: "Charles, I've been hoping to have a chance to talk to you. I've been watching the pair of you and I think there are a few things that you are too young to understand by yourself but that you probably ought to know," and then make as much as possible of the conversation, and of my own role as wise and sympathetic counselor. Cara does none of this. Lightly, almost in passing, she hands him names for the stings that before long will make their presence felt amid his honeyed happiness: the romantic infatuation that flavors their friendship, Sebastian's troubled relationship with his family, and his increasingly problematic drinking. Then, showing no curiosity about his reaction,

1. Waugh, *Brideshead Revisited*, 101.

no need for engagement, gratitude, or even acknowledgment, she lightly turns the conversation away, "saying in fond, mocking tones, 'How good it is to sit in the shade and talk of love.'"[2] I often look to this conversation, and try to emulate Cara's self-effacing lightness of touch, to offer whatever I have to offer and to look for nothing in return deeper than the noisy youthful company of the moment, to learn the art of balance, the discipline of being present, available and interested, but not intrusive, always poised to recede silently when I am no longer needed.

Having students in and out is a great pleasure, and like all great pleasures can turn sour or even dangerous if not bounded by sharp self-awareness and careful discipline. "Teach us to care and not to care," T. S. Eliot writes. "Teach us to sit still." It's easy for me to care for and about the students whose lives send them our way; it's harder not to care about our own place in their lives and loyalties, to sit still when they close the chapter of life in which we figured. But I know, from bitter experience, that if I cling to them, my hospitality is a facade: hostility and control rather than true welcome.

It is altogether possible that the lessons I have learned about letting beloved students go their way is merely a preparation for a greater letting go. The chapter in which there are young people showing up near midnight and cooking themselves eggs without a by-your-leave may close too. We're getting older: in the last few years we've moved into the age range of our students' parents. Our own children are getting older: before long, they will move into the age range of our students. The current state of affairs, as dearly as I love it, and as deeply as it defines my life, may not last much longer. At present it looks as if Robby and his crowd are being succeeded, gradually and organically, by another group. That's what has always happened so far and I hope it will keep happening. On the other hand, these might be the last to decide to make themselves at home here. Should that be the case I will have to call on whatever balance and discipline I have acquired

2. Ibid. 103.

over the years to help me bid an uncomplaining and gracious goodbye to this bright, noisy, and joyful phase of our lives, to sit still as young lives swirl past ours and out into their own, and to discern where God will next invite me.

Bibliography

L'Abri Fellowship International. "L'Abri Today." http://www.labri.org/today. html.

"The Aims and Means of the Catholic Worker." Online: http://www. catholicworker.org/aimsandmeanstext.cfm?number=5.

L'Arche USA. "L'Arche USA."

Augustine. *Confessions.* Translated by Henry Chadwick. Oxford: Oxford University Press, 1991.

————. *On Christian Doctrine.* Translated by D. W. Robertson. New York: Macmillan, 1958.

————. *The Usefulness of Belief.* In *Augustine: Earlier Writings.* Selected and translated by John H. S. Burleigh. Philadelphia: Westminster, 1953.

Dawkins, Richard. *The God Delusion.* Boston: Houghton Mifflin, 2006.

Day, Dorothy. *House of Hospitality.* City: Sheed & Ward, 1939.

Dinesen, Isak. "Babette's Feast." In *Anecdotes of Destiny and Ehrengard.* New York: Vintage, 1993.

Ehrman, Bart D. *God's Problem: How the Bible Fails to Answer Our Most Important Question—Why We Suffer.* New York: HarperOne, 2008.

Eliot, George. *Middlemarch.* New York: Bantam, 1992.

Lewis, C. S. *The Great Divorce.* New York: Touchstone, 1996.

————. *Surprised by Joy: The Shape of My Early Life.* San Diego: Harcourt Brace Jovanovich, 1984.

Oden, Amy G., editor. *And You Welcomed Me: A Sourcebook on Hospitality in Early Christianity.* Nashville: Abingdon, 2001.

Pohl, Christine. *Making Room: Recovering Hospitality as a Christian Tradition.* Grand Rapids: Eerdmans, 1999.

Proust, Marcel. *Remembrance of Things Past.* Translated by C. K. Scott Moncrieff and Terence Kilmartin. Vol. 1, *Swann's Way.* New York: Random House, 1981.

Schaeffer, Edith. *L'Abri.* 2nd ed. Wheaton, IL: Crossway, 1992.

Vanier, Jean. *Community and Growth.* London: Darton Longman & Todd, 1979.

Waugh, Evelyn. *Brideshead Revisited.* Boston: Little, Brown, 1945.

Wojtyla, Karol. *Love and Responsibility.* Rev. ed. Translated by H. T. Willetts. San Francisco: Ignatius, 1993.